25 Years of Ed Tech

T0345247

Issues in Distance Education
SERIES EDITOR: *George Veletsianos*

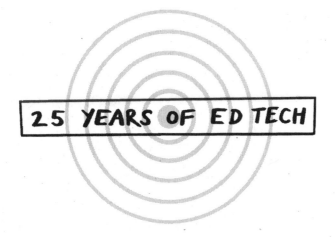

25 YEARS OF ED TECH

Martin Weller

AU PRESS

Published by AU Press, Athabasca University
1200, 10011 - 109 Street, Edmonton, AB T5J 3S8
https://doi.org/10.15215/aupress/9781771993050.01

Cover design and interior art by Bryan Mathers, Visual Thinkery
Interior design by Natalie Olsen
Printed and bound in Canada

Library and Archives Canada Cataloguing in Publication
Title: 25 years of ed tech / Martin Weller.
Other titles: Twenty-five years of ed tech
Names: Weller, Martin, author.
Series: Issues in distance education series.
Description: Series statement: Issues in distance education series |
Includes bibliographical references.
Identifiers: Canadiana (print) 20200152211 | Canadiana (ebook) 20200152238 |
ISBN 9781771993050 (softcover) | ISBN 9781771993067 (pdf) | ISBN 9781771993074 (epub)
ISBN 9781771993081 (Kindle)
Subjects: LCSH: Educational technology. | LCSH: Education, Higher.
Classification: LCC LB1028.3 .W45 2020 | DDC 371.33—dc23

We acknowledge the financial assistance provided by the Government of Alberta
through the Alberta Media Fund.

To my two canine writing buddies,
Teilo and Bruno, on whose walks most of
the ideas in this book were developed,
and who listened patiently to my
musings on MOOC and metadata.

CONTENTS

ACKNOWLEDGEMENTS

One of the themes of this book is the emergence of a critical voice in educational technology, which emphasizes the human and social role of ed tech. Histories of technology are often dominated by male inventor stories, and as a counter to this, I would like to acknowledge the important work of many women in educational technology. The following writers and researchers have all had a significant impact on my own thinking and more broadly helped shift the dialogue in educational technology away from an unquestioning technological solutionism and male culture. Educational technology is at a key juncture in its development, and if it is to continue to benefit learners, educators, and society more generally, then the presence of such voices will be essential. I would like to thank Maha Bali, Sian Bayne, Helen Beetham, Frances Bell, Kate Bowles, Lorna Campbell, Amanda Coolidge, Catherine Cronin, Laura Czerniewicz, Maren Deepwell, Robin DeRosa, Josie Fraser, Cheryl Hodgkinson-Williams, Donna Lanclos, Diana Laurillard, Tressie MacMillan Cottom, Sheila MacNeill, Tannis Morgan, Joyce Seitzinger, Bonnie Stewart, and Audrey Watters, among many, many others. Their work has made ed tech a better place for everyone.

In addition, I would like to offer my thanks to George Veletsianos, Connor Houlihan, and all the staff at Athabasca University Press who have provided such excellent advice and help in bringing this book to publication and for making open access book publishing a reality.

25 Years of Ed Tech

YEAR ZERO

The Historical Amnesia of Ed Tech

An opinion often proffered amongst educational technology (ed tech) professionals is that theirs is a fast-changing field. This statement is sometimes used as a motivation (or veiled threat) to senior managers to embrace ed tech because if they miss out now, it'll be too late to catch up later, or more drastically, they will face extinction. For example, Rigg (2014) asked "can universities survive the digital age?" in an article that argues universities are too slow to be relevant to young people who are embedded in their fast-moving, digital age. Such accounts both underestimate the degree to which universities have changed and are capable of change while also overestimating the digital natives-type account that all students want a university to be the equivalent of Instagram. Fullick (2014) highlighted that this imperative to adopt all change unquestioningly, and adopt it now, has a distinctly Darwinian undertone: "Resistance to change is presented as resistance to what is natural and inevitable" (para. 3). An essential ingredient in this narrative is that higher education does not change, and is incapable of change, therefore change must be forced upon it. Ed tech is the means by which this change-or-die narrative is realized, with people often divided, or forced, into pro- or anti-camps regarding any technology-based adaptation in higher education. Ed tech, then, is not a peripheral interest in higher education but is increasingly framed as the manner in which the future of all higher education will be determined. One aim of this book, then, is to provide some antidote to the narrative of higher education's inability to change by illustrating both the breadth of change and innovation that has occurred in higher education over the past 25 years, and also to draw attention to examples when the caution and desire to examine evidence has been correctly applied.

Amid this breathless attempt to keep abreast of new developments, the ed tech field is also remarkably poor at recording its own history and reflecting critically on its development, as if there is no time to look in the rear-view mirror in a field that is always interested in the future. When ed tech critic Audrey Watters (2018a) put out a request for recommended books on the history of educational technology, I couldn't suggest any beyond the handful she already had listed. There are ed tech books that often start with a historical chapter to set the current work in context, and there are ed tech books that are now a part of history, but there are very few that deal specifically with the field's history. Maybe this reflects a lack of interest, as there has always been something of a year-zero mentality in the field. Ed tech is also an area which people move into from other disciplines, so there is no shared set of concepts or history. This can be liberating but also infuriating; for instance, I'm sure I wasn't alone in emitting the occasional sigh of exasperation when during the massive open online courses (MOOC) rush of 2012, so many "new" discoveries about online learning were reported — discoveries that were already tired concepts in the ed tech field. A second aim of this book, then, is to provide one contribution to a literature of educational technology history.

In 2018 the UK's Association for Learning Technology (ALT) celebrated its 25th anniversary, and to commemorate this I undertook a blog series on 25 Years of Ed Tech. As well as providing a discussion point for many in the association and their experience with ed tech (e.g., Thomas, 2018), it was also a useful time frame to revisit. The period 1994–2018 (inclusive) represents what we may think of as the Internet years of ed tech. There were some applications of the Internet prior to this, with e-learning dating from the late 1980s, and there are many applications that can still be classified as ed tech that are not reliant on the Internet during this period, but the mid-1990s witnessed the shift to the Internet being the dominant technology shaping ed tech. Indeed, an alternative title for this book might be "Educational Technology: The Internet Years."

There are many different ways to approach a recent history of ed tech; for instance, it could be based around themes, individuals, semantic analysis of conference papers, surveys, and so on. For this book and the blog series, I have taken the straightforward approach of selecting a different educational technology, theory, or concept for each of the years from 1994 through to, and including, 2018. This is not (just) an exercise in historical pedantry to combat the claims from the latest ed tech start-up to have "invented" a particular approach, but it allows us to examine what has changed, what remains the same, and what general patterns can be discerned from this history. It is also an attempt to give some shared historical basis to the field of ed tech. The final entry in this book focuses on what I have termed "ed tech's dystopian turn," as there has been a shift from often unquestioning advocacy of particular technologies to a more critical, theoretical understanding. This represents something of a maturing in the field, although many technology vendor conferences are still free of any such critique. Ed tech itself, then, is at an interesting point in its development, perhaps akin to that of the discipline of art history in the postwar years. The 1970s, in particular, saw the development of what became termed "New Art History," which the *Concise Oxford Dictionary of Art Terms* (Clark, 2010) defines as follows:

> Something of an umbrella term, embracing elements of Marxism, semiotics, and deconstruction, it is generally used to describe the various approaches to art history as an intellectual discipline which developed after the Second World War. This occurred in reaction to the earlier, predominantly literary and Renaissance-based tradition of art-historical scholarship which was widely perceived to have dominated the subject and to have become increasingly irrelevant to the modern world. (para. 1)

Prior to this, art history had largely been concerned with the lives of individual artists, but critics such as Hadjinicolaou (1978) argued that this approach proved an obstacle to art history as a serious field of study, while others such as Pollock (1988) highlighted how such an approach necessarily privileged a male perspective. This reappraisal of what it meant to be engaged in art history led to an expansion in models applied to the field, such as those mentioned in the definition above. Art history essentially shifted from being the study of the history of artists to the study of the role of art itself.

The history of ed tech can also be said to be focused on inventors, as Kernohan (2014) puts it, "Birth myths ... are ahistorical. They tie in with a phallogocentrism of the concept of creation as a single act by a single person (generally a man ...) rather than a whole set of pre-existing conditions and preoccupations" (para. 4). This is the grounding of the year-zero mentality, where any recognition of prior work undermines the myth of the individual genius creator. In a modest way, then, I hope this book provides one tool for allowing a similar critical turn in ed tech, by highlighting the long history and repeated attempts that underlie many technologies.

Looking back 25 years starts in 1994, when the web was just about to garner mainstream attention. It was accessed through dial-up modems, and there was a general sense of puzzlement about what it would mean, both for society more generally and for higher education in particular. Some academics considered it to be a fad. One colleague dismissed my idea of a fully online course by declaring, "No one wants to study like that." But the potential of the web for higher education was clear, even if the direction this would take over the next 25 years was unpredictable.

Although the selection in this book is largely a personal and subjective one, it should resonate in some places with most practitioners in the field. I am guilty of also being rather arbitrary in allocating a specific year to any given technology: the selected year is not when a particular technology was invented but, rather, when it became — in my view — significant. The result of this approach is that inevitably you will find yourself disagreeing with my selection at some point on three grounds. The first point of disagreement is the exclusion of technologies that should have been included. By only allowing myself one ed tech development per year, the range is limited, and it is also, admittedly, biased by my own experience. I acknowledge that mobile learning, game-based learning, and learning design all merit entries in here, but are absent. As with lists such as "Best 100 films" or similar, they are as much characterized by what they leave out as what they include. In addition, there are limitations in the "one technology a year" method; it tends to prioritize technology, for example, as these are easier elements to hook onto, and it is also not very suitable for longer, horizontal themes, such as accessibility. This could run through many of the applications, so the web, associated e-learning standards, open educational resources (OER), Second Life, massive open online courses (MOOC), and so on, all have an accessibility strand. This, and other broader issues, such as academic labour, the concept of identity, and the role of the university can be glimpsed in places in this book, but probably merit a "25 Years of…" account of their own.

The second point of disagreement will likely be which particular year I have chosen to allocate to any specific technology. You will undoubtedly feel that some should have come earlier or later. This is partly an issue of logistics, in that some years saw several technologies vie for inclusion and so they had to be spread across two or more. It is also a result of perception, because I have opted for "significance" as my criterion rather than year of invention, and this is a subjective interpretation, and one that may also be influenced by geographical location — I am based in the UK and some technologies will be deemed significant later or earlier in that context than elsewhere. The third point of disagreement may come in the form of the treatment given to any specific entry. For this, I plead brevity of entry, as any one of these topics warrants, and indeed has, several volumes dedicated to them. The aim of each short chapter is to provide an overview, to supply some relevant research, and to draw out general themes that can be synthesized in the final chapter. I hope that even with these three disagreements likely to arise there is nevertheless something useful in the book for most readers.

One small example of the aim of this book can be represented by analysis of a single quote from Internet expert Clay Shirky (2012). Talking about MOOC (the subject of chapter 19 in this book) during their peak in 2012, he predicted that "higher education is now being disrupted; our MP3 is the massive open online course (or mooc), and our Napster is Udacity, the education startup" (para. 8).

Napster was the file-sharing service that started the online music revolution and Udacity was the first MOOC company. I could have selected from any number of quotes from a range of ed tech futurologists, but this one is telling and gets at the motivations for writing this book. Firstly, it is (perhaps wilfully) ignorant of the long history of e-learning at universities and posits that MOOC are the first flush of online learning. This in itself highlights the need for a broader recognition of the use of ed tech in higher education. Secondly, given this history of e-learning implementation, the quote is not so much about the technology of MOOC, but rather the Silicon Valley-type business model being applied to higher education. It was the large-scale interest of venture capitalists and a seemingly palpable example of the much-loved disruption myth (although, as usual, these predictions proved to be false) that generated much of the media interest. What this book hopes to set forth is that, while the start-up-based culture is certainly one model of ed tech innovation, it is not the *only* model. By first ignoring its own history, and then allowing a dominant narrative to displace it, higher education fails to make the case that there is another model, which operates to different demands, timescales, and metrics. Thirdly, this combination of historical ignorance and imposed narrative necessitates that much of the existing knowledge established over years of practice and research is ignored. In order for disruption to take place, and Udacity to be "our" Napster, it is a requirement that the incumbents in an industry (in this case, universities and colleges) are incapable of engaging with the new technology and unaware of its implications. The history of ed tech set out in this book refutes this narrative.

These will be themes that will recur throughout the book and be explored in greater detail, but this one typical quote in itself demonstrates the purpose, and I would suggest, need, for books such as this. In conclusion, then, the aims of this book are fivefold:

- To provide *a* (but definitely not *the*) basis for shared understanding and common knowledge between practitioners who enter into the ed tech field.

- To demonstrate a history of innovation and effective implementation of ed tech in higher education.

- To draw out themes and lessons from the application of different educational technologies over an extended time period that can helpfully shape future implementation.

- To highlight the necessity of a critical approach in ed tech.

- To provide an alternative historical narrative for ed tech to counteract the year zero, disruption based one.

Whether it is successful in meeting these, I will leave you to judge. If it is not, then simply being an exercise in historical pedantry is an acceptable outcome for the author.

CHAPTER 01

1994

Bulletin Board Systems

As well as being the convenient 25-year point, 1994 also marks an interesting shift in educational technology. I work at the Institute of Educational Technology at the Open University (OU), and for much of its life hitherto the focus of research was on the effectiveness of analog technology. The sort of questions researchers sought to address were: How could the text in printed units be effectively formatted to encourage interaction between the reader and the text? What is the best use of video or audio cassettes within a course structure? How effective were residential summer schools? And so on. By 1994 the shift was more to digital content—multimedia CD-ROMs, and, as we shall see, some nascent online tools. So, 1994 provides a useful starting point for plotting the development of what many now consider to be the definition of educational technology—the use of Internet-related technology in education. However, given my complaints in the introduction about the historical amnesia of educational technology, it would be amiss of me to suggest that the online version of ed tech is the only one. But it is in 1994 that this account begins, and the focus is thenceforth almost exclusively on technologies that are online or radically altered by the possibility of digital, networked approaches.

In 1994 the web was just about to enter mainstream consciousness, and the Internet was gaining more popularity. One of the technologies that old ed tech practitioners express nostalgia for is the Bulletin Board System (BBS). These were really the forerunner for much of what we know as social media and developed the structures and processes (or lack of them) for discussion forums. The BBS operated in a world of dial-up modem connections. Each one acted in effect as its own server, and each user would connect directly to the BBS. This meant that the number of concurrent users was limited, and also that those users tended to want to get online and off again quickly (in the early days you were still paying for connection minutes, like a regular phone call). While they were briefly connected, users would upload, download, and send email, but from our perspective the most interesting part was posting to public message boards. Initially designed to be analogous to the cork bulletin board people would be familiar with, they soon divided into specialist groups and discussion forums. Systems such as FidoNet allowed users to connect to different BBS so they could communicate with millions of people globally. As Internet access became more affordable, the underlying server structure of BBS changed. People could now access BBS from anywhere in the world, for equal cost, but the conventions and communications practices they had developed persisted, and were modelled by Internet service providers such as AOL and CompuServe.

These nascent online discussion forums marked the first real awareness of education to the possibility of the Internet. They often required specialist software at this stage, were text-based, and, because they relied on expensive dial-up, the ability to sync offline was important. But suddenly the possibility for remote students to engage in discussions with others was not out of the question for the average student. The language used to refer to these systems highlights their novelty and that they were occurring in an age when analog dominated. So, they are referred to as "electronic" bulletin board systems, or multi-user systems. Neither of these terms would require specifying now, which is indicative of the large cultural shift that has taken place since their inception.

At the OU they were experimenting with a BBS called CoSy. While some could see their potential, they were still viewed as a very niche application. At the time, the university needed to help people with the entire process of getting online, acting as an Internet service provider, dealing with unfamiliar software and advice on how to communicate appropriately online. This uses up a lot of academic real estate in a course about, say, Shakespeare. The following quote (Mason & Kaye, 1989) about the use of the CoSy system highlights that students did not always share educators' enthusiasm for the benefits of the technology:

> A series of questions about the convenience of electronic communications was included in the questionnaire for the course database. These show that about 60–70% of students returning questionnaires found [online communication] less effective for contacting their tutor, getting help, socializing and saving time and money in travelling. (p. 123)

The application of BBS was often reserved for subjects where the medium was the message: for example, in courses on technology and communication, and even then, students often found the technology frustrating. Despite the inevitable early teething problems, particularly for distance education, the possibilities were revolutionary — BBS had the potential to effectively remove the distance element. The only way students communicated with each other previously was at summer school and in face-to-face tutorials, or via telephone with their tutor. At campus-based universities, BBS were often used in computer labs, for example, to deliver early forms of e-learning, and in this sense can be viewed as the precursor to the Learning Management System (LMS) or Virtual Learning Environment (VLE). Levine (2018) recalled the use of BBS on campus in colleges during the 1990s, saying they "offered a suite of self-paced classes delivered over the network called 'Open Entry / Open Exit' ... [and] tools for writing/submitting assignments, holding discussions, open class and direct communications" (paras. 3–4). As we shall see with later technologies, the early users of BBS tended to be already well educated, and had above-average earnings (James, Wotring, & Forrest, 1995). This was because they were a niche interest, and required specialist, often expensive, equipment to access. But as we know, if we view platforms such as Facebook as the successors to

BBS, this privileged demographic did not persist. This is worth noting because new developments in ed tech, such as MOOC and OER, also reveal a similar user demographic. The question is whether this is permanent or a phase that leads to wider adoption.

Other early indicators that BBS provided that would be significant for ed tech included issues of distributing copyrighted material, Elkin-Koren (1994) arguing that restrictive copyright laws were preventing BBS from becoming effective social forums; the development of online communities, particularly for groups which might be marginalized in conventional society (Correll, 1995); the development of support groups as a means of bringing together geographically dispersed people with specialist interests (e.g., Benton, 1996; Finn & Lavitt, 1994); and conflicts between freedom of speech, libel, and online abuse (Weber, 1995). These are amplified now and society-wide, but their seeds are all evident in the early applications of BBS.

The lessons from BBS are that some technologies have very specific applications, some die out, and others morph to a universal application. BBS did the latter, but in 1994, most people thought this technology would be in one of the first two categories. What was required for it to become a mainstream part of the educational technology landscape was the technical and social infrastructure that removed the high technical barrier to implementation.

CHAPTER 02

1995

The Web

While the web was actually invented in 1989, the focus of this book is not on when a technology was invented, but rather when it became relevant in ed tech, which usually results from a certain level of uptake. While the story of the invention of the web is reasonably well known, it is worth revisiting with the knowledge of how it developed, and to identify the foundations in that development that have come to shape so much of educational technology.

Unlike many origin stories where claims are disputed, there is a clear and acknowledged inventor of the web — Sir Tim Berners-Lee. In 1989, he was working as a software engineer at the large particle physics laboratory, CERN. With scientists from around the world working on different projects and generating large amounts of data and findings, Berners-Lee (n.d.) identified that they had difficulty in sharing information:

> In those days, there was different information on different computers, but you had to log on to different computers to get at it. Also, sometimes you had to learn a different program on each computer. Often it was just easier to go and ask people when they were having coffee. (para. 1)

Although Berners-Lee is the acknowledged inventor of the web, he was not operating in a vacuum. His proposal (Berners-Lee, 1989) brought together the Internet as a means of linking computers, and hypertext as a method of writing linked documents. By 1990 Berners-Lee had developed four technologies that made the web functional and that still underpin it:

HTML: Hypertext Markup Language, an easy to use markup language to produce web documents.

URI: Uniform Resource Identifier (also known as URL), a means of giving any page or resource on the web a unique address so it can be linked to and located.

HTTP: Hypertext Transfer Protocol, a data transfer method that allows web resources to be retrieved across the Internet.

Web browser: a piece of software that utilizes the previous three technologies to allow a user to navigate and use the web.

The fundamental design principles were as significant as the specific technologies in the development of the web. Berners-Lee (1989) identified that for success any such system needed to be open, and not a proprietary system owned by any one corporation. The technical attributes of the web can also be seen as giving rise to its social attributes. It was designed as a communication system, around principles of robustness, decentralization and openness. In terms of robustness, the web was built on the Internet, which was designed to survive attack, failure, or sabotage of any particular part and still function as a meaningful communication system, in other words as a network system, with no centralized, and thus vulnerable, control. This aspect is fundamental to how the web shaped society. With a decentralized system, no single node is, theoretically, more important than any other. Inherent in this is a democratization of communication. Although the ability to pay for search engine results and game algorithms would skew this, in principle the web page that any individual publishes is as significant as those from any large corporation, news outlet, or government. An open system, therefore, follows from the decentralized approach, so any compatible computer can connect and participate.

From these technological features, then, a system evolved which had no central authority, meaning that it was difficult for established agencies to control what was published on the web. What anyone could publish and debate was not governed or censored. In many ways, the Internet acts like a living organism, driven by these social values, and in this both the potential for good and ill was established. Much of this book will explore how these features developed in educational terms.

By 1995, the web browser was becoming reasonably commonplace, with Netscape dominating. With Facebook pages and WordPress sites created at the click of a button now, it is difficult to remember the effort but also the magic in creating your first web page using hand-coded HTML. I used to run Open University summer school sessions where we taught people HTML and over the course of a morning got them to publish a page online. The realization that anyone in the world could now see their page was a revelation. This act now seems like the mythical mudskipper crawling from the sea to the land: a symbolic evolutionary moment.

At this stage, the web still required a degree of technical expertise and was awkward to use, but it was on the way to becoming easy enough, and sufficiently interesting, to be moving beyond pure specialist interest. People regularly made proclamations that nobody would shop online, or that it was the equivalent of CB radio. Even at the time, these views seemed misguided: we could not predict smart phones and ubiquitous Wi-Fi but being able to dial up and connect to information sources anywhere was always going to be revolutionary — and particularly so for education. What the web browser provided (although it would take a few years to materialize) was a common tool so that specific software was no longer required for every function that you sought to carry out online. Prior to this file transfer was performed through File Transfer Protocol (FTP), email through specific clients, bulletin board systems through software such as FidoNet, and so on. The browser provided the potential to unify all these, and more, in one tool. In this the browser was like the HTML specification that underpinned it — in many ways it was inferior to bespoke versions for any specific function, but its generality made it good enough. This was one reason that many tech people failed to appreciate the significance of the web, they could always point out the superior functionality of their favoured software tool. Unix geeks sniffed at the simplicity of the web compared with what they could realize through command language interfaces. But "good enough" is usually the victor in terms of popularity if it can be made universal — Facebook is a more recent example of this phenomenon.

Learning to hand-code HTML presented a significant barrier to the popular adoption of the web. However, web publishing tools such as FrontPage emerged, which allowed people to use templates and simple menu functions, and then click "publish." More broadly, Angelfire and GeoCities were online providers that helped people create websites with their templated tools. Many universities ran a default service for staff to generate their own pages. These were nearly always based on Unix servers, and because of the way the file structure was specified in Unix, each user had their own directory which was accessible by typing ~. Hence universities ran "tilde" servers, with web addresses such as www.uni.ac.uk/~mweller. A certain university style developed for these rather vanilla websites, which sometimes persist to this day.

Even in this simple design, the nascent possibilities of the web for education were evident. Firstly, it made communication, and as a result, networking, much easier. Even though social media didn't exist yet, it was still possible to find the work of a scholar at another university and send them an email. This was, by some distance, easier than relying on an introduction or adopting the more intrusive and less reliable method of telephoning. Secondly, the uploading of publications to your own website marked the beginning of consideration about the dissemination of knowledge and the relationship with publishers which would lead to much of the open access developments. Thirdly, academics began to share teaching resources in this way, which as with publications, would plant the seeds of the open education movement.

Therefore, in this early, often amateurish, development of what became known as Web 1.0 we can see the important aspects of what the web gave education — the freedom to publish, communicate, and share. For distance education, which had previously relied on expensive broadcast (the much loved OU BBC programs, for instance) or shipping physical copies of books, videos, and CDs, this was a significant change. It not only altered how single function distance education institutions such as the OU operated, but also lowered the cost of entry into the distance education market, so now all other universities could effectively become distance, or hybrid, education providers.

The web laid the foundation for nearly all the technologies that follow in this book and is the one we are still feeling the impact of most keenly. Much of ed tech is essentially a variant on the question: what does the web mean for us? In teaching, the development of LMS, OER, and MOOC, as well as related pedagogic approaches, are all examples of this. In research, the use of blogs, analytics, and Web 2.0 tools have all been significant. For academics and universities responding to the cultural shifts caused by social media, video, and the dark side of the web has become strategically important. The removal of the publication filter that the web provided was often touted as the most significant socio-technological change since the invention of the printing press (e.g., Giles, 1996) and, 25 years later, that view does not seem like hyperbole.

CHAPTER 03

1996

Computer-Mediated Communication

Computer-mediated communication (CMC) should be viewed as the larger category incorporating Bulletin Board Systems and other forms of online communication. The reason for revisiting some of the area covered by Bulletin Board Systems (BBS) with the concept of CMC is that it represents a good example of how a technology develops into a more generic educational approach. CMC became a popular phrase around 1996 and represents higher education beginning to engage with online tools in a more meaningful theoretical, conceptual manner, comparable to the way higher education had engaged with early developments in conventional open and distance education, when there had been considerable research on the pedagogic implications of educating in this manner. CMC has a broad definition of various forms of human communication that is conducted through networked computers. It is usually divided into two main formats of synchronous, i.e., occurring in real time, and asynchronous, i.e., not restricted to simultaneous timing. The types of CMC technologies back in 1996 included instant messaging, email, BBS, early Voice over Internet Protocol (VoIP) and video systems (precursors to the likes of Skype), online databases, discussion forums, and even online multi-user games (the Multi-User Dungeon [MUD] being an early form of distributed online gaming).

The adoption of CMC was particularly driven by a shift from purely text-based systems to graphical interfaces which made them easier to use. For instance, the Open University (OU) switched from the text-based CoSy system to the graphical FirstClass system (https://en.wikipedia.org/wiki/FirstClass). As well as being more user friendly, these systems also had sophisticated administrative back-end systems that allowed the automatic allocation of students to groups, multiple roles with a range of different permissions, offline synchronization, threading to structure conversations, and a high degree of personalization for users. This highlights the shift to a more educational focus in the deployment of CMC and tools developed with education more specifically as a target market.

Such systems were forerunners to LMS, both technically and culturally. Many CMC systems were simple enough to use for most students that the pedagogic benefits could now be realized. This is again a recurrent ed tech theme — when the barriers to the use of a particular technology become low enough (and in the case of smart phones, say, almost invisible) that its use can be generalized, then it gains broad acceptance across disciplines. From CMC, a number of approaches and concepts were derived that would inform much of the e-learning developments that would follow, including online tutor groups, e-moderation (Salmon, 2004), forums, online conferences, netiquette, and so on. What CMC brought to the fore was the need to develop models for how this technology could be used effectively across multiple subject domains. For example, online tutor groups are not the same as face-to-face tutor groups, they require a different set of behaviours to be learned by students and educators and activities need to be structured accordingly. With CMC, asynchronous online group work became a possibility, but at the same time, it was also a very frustrating experience for students. A collaborative activity that could usually be completed in an afternoon in a face-to-face setting would probably occupy students for three weeks or so when completing it online and asynchronously. It required that they introduce themselves, establish roles, allocate work, conduct the work, and then combine it.

The social elements in these tasks can happen in a short time frame when in a face-to-face setting ("Who wants to be the project manager? Okay, you do it."), but can stretch over days when people are communicating asynchronously, perhaps lack the social cues to interact, are waiting for responses, or if someone may be offline for an extended period. It is probably the case that as educators many of us became rather overenthusiastic about the new communication possibilities, and I have sympathy with the student on one of my early online courses who bemoaned, "It was a new collaborative activity every week!" This work in online collaboration, however, was driven by a strong theoretical underpinning, drawing on pedagogic and communication research, particularly in the area of constructivism (see chapter 4). Gradually the viability of online teaching via CMC gained credibility until it became the norm for many.

If the benefit of the web was the removal of barriers to broadcast and publishing, then CMC delivered the ability to collaborate at a distance. This is arguably more powerful in education than the democratization of broadcast, but it also gets to the heart of different views about education. The use of the web to disseminate information cheaply to a mass audience was represented by what can be termed the "infinite lecture hall" model, whereby large numbers of students could be taught relatively cheaply, because the cost of delivering content to 10,000 students was largely the same as delivering it to 10 students if it was based around a broadcast model. The use of the Internet to facilitate collaboration and discussion in groups at a distance emphasizes a more student focused, less industrial model. In such a model, there is more dialogue between students, but this requires moderation and support. Student dialogue forms a much greater part of these courses—in a conventional course, the educator accounts for approximately 80% of the dialogue, whereas CMC structured courses have only 10–15% of dialogue attributable to the educator (Jonassen, Davidson, Collins, Campbell, & Haag, 1995). Therefore, this student exchange cannot be "captured" beforehand in the way a conventional lecture can but needs to be facilitated during the course itself. The costs associated with e-learning will be examined in chapter 8, but the difference between these approaches was highlighted by Bates (1995) who analyzed several costs associated with the broadcast model versus the communication model. Adopting a cost per student study-hour model he found that the broadcast (or in the terminology of the time, computer-based training, CBT) models were characterized by high initial fixed costs associated with development or purchase, but low variable costs — hence the infinite lecture hall model since adding more students did not noticeably increase costs. A more CMC-based course, however, showed that the

> total costs rise directly with student numbers. There is relatively little front-end investment in these courses, and if interactivity, a major feature of CMC, is to be effective, the number of instructors increases with the number of students. Instructors are the main cost with this technology. (Bates, 1995, p. 223)

In this we see another common theme in which technology brings underlying beliefs regarding education into focus and exaggerates them. These two fundamental models are still behind many of the different approaches in ed tech; for example, the two different models of MOOC that we will see in chapter 19 are termed "xMOOC" and "cMOOC" and map closely onto broadcast and communication models, respectively.

CMC then, building on BBS, raised the significance of communication. This is again one of the recurring themes in ed tech, that the implementation of technology makes people evaluate what is core in education itself, which had hitherto been implicit. When CMC became more mainstream, then it required educators to explicitly design communication into their courses. When it occurred online, it didn't "just happen," or rather it can't be assumed to just arise as it does in face-to-face, informal settings. When there was no alternative to face-to-face settings, the function of communication was not considered in such detail, but in fact, when analyzed, universities were designed specifically to foreground effective communication. Students were brought together in one physical location, over a tightly constrained time frame, with a strict timetable which occurs within an architecture that offers students multiple spaces (cafes, bars, common areas) and opportunities for informal discussion. This is all obvious in retrospect, but it was so commonplace that the intentionality of the structure became invisible. But when the online element was introduced, educators were forced to consider how they either replicated these interactions or improved upon them.

CMC raises the following sorts of questions: When should we explicitly direct communication between students? How do we facilitate this? Should it be assessed? If so, how? How does the learning environment inhibit, or encourage this type of communication? How does the design of the course encourage the type of informal discussion that aids so much of campus-based education? And so on. For most educators when they become new lecturers at a traditional face-to-face university, I suspect these types of questions are not really asked of their educational approach–it is assumed within the architecture, timetabling, and structure of the physical campus. When that education moves online, then these questions are pertinent not just for the technologized version of a course but for the original face-to-face one too.

This is one of the often unspoken, and largely intangible, benefits of ed tech — that it surfaces assumptions in existing practice that bear analysis. This led to a wealth of research, experimentation, and theorizing, which continues to this day.

CHAPTER 04

1997

Constructivism

By 1997, web-based learning was gaining a lot of attention, and with this focus people began to search around for new models of teaching. Simply recreating the lecture model online was problematic in a period when bandwidth limitations meant that streaming video was not a realistic option for many. More significantly, the advent of the web seemed revolutionary, and for those educators who were keen to exploit its potential, there was a desire to utilize the characteristics that the web brought to the fore and not simply recreate the existing model. These characteristics included communication, access to different knowledge sources, non-linear narratives created through hyperlinking, and democratization of publishing. To fully realize this potential, it seemed obvious that a different model from the conventional lecture-centred one would be required. Later interpretations of online learning, particularly MOOC, have reverted to an instructivist, lecture-based model, which indicates its resilience as an approach, but it also highlights that the technological limitations of the early web forced educators to search for a different model. Had the ubiquitous broadband been available in 1997, maybe the early e-learning models would have been less innovative. In order to represent this pedagogical thinking that the arrival of the web inspired, the selection for 1997, therefore, is not a technology but rather an educational theory.

Constructivism was by no means new in 1997, dating back to Piaget, Vygotsky, and Bruner. Piaget (1964) proposed the processes by which learners (particularly children) construct knowledge. This can be seen as a reaction against the behaviourist models created by psychologists such as Skinner (1963). Constructivism emphasizes the experience and role of the individual in developing concepts. Vygotsky (1978) developed this concept further with the idea of social constructivism: the proposition that learning is not an individual exercise but is developed through social interaction and couched in language. An influential notion from Vygotsky for many constructivists is the "zone of proximal development" (ZPD), which is the difference between what a learner can do with help, what they can do unaided, and what they cannot do. The ZPD is where a learner can progress if they are aided by an educator. This highlights the social and dialogic aspects of learning by emphasizing the interaction between educators and learners. From this, Bruner in particular (Wood, Bruner, & Ross, 1976; Bruner, 1978) developed the concept of "scaffolding," which can be seen as points, actions, and support methods that allow a learner to work effectively in the ZPD. Scaffolding was a key concept in the early adoption of web-based learning, as it seemed to offer a model for helping learners through this new environment, without resorting to very prescribed, didactic approaches.

The principal concept of constructivism, then, is that learners construct their own knowledge, based on their experience and relationship with concepts, often through some form of social interaction. Jonassen (1991) described it thus:

> Constructivism ... claims that reality is constructed by the knower based upon mental activity. Humans are perceivers and interpreters who construct their own reality through engaging in those mental activities. ... What the mind produces are mental models that explain to the knower what he or she has perceived .... We all conceive of the external reality somewhat differently, based on our unique set of experiences with the world and our beliefs about them. (p. 6)

It's a (sometimes vague) learning theory rather than a specific pedagogy, so how it is implemented varies. It has often been put into practice by active learning, or discovery-based approaches. The appeal of this for online learning is the sense that the web gave agency to learners—they could create, collaborate, and discover for themselves, freed from the conventions of time and distance. When people can learn anywhere and anytime, then the pedagogy designed for a lecture hall seems limiting.

A commonly used phrase at the time was that constructivism, and in particular constructivist approaches delivered online, saw a fundamental shift in the role of the educator from "the sage on the stage" to the "guide on the side." King (1993) summarized this transformation thus:

> In contrast to the transmittal model illustrated by the classroom lecture-note taking scenario, the constructivist model places students at the center of the process—actively participating in thinking and discussing ideas while making meaning for themselves. And the professor, instead of being the "sage on the stage," functions as a "guide on the side," facilitating learning in less directive ways. (p. 31)

It was a neat, if overused, phrase and certainly came with a set of value judgments about the "transmittal" model that were not fully justified. The concept of placing the student at "the centre" of the learning process is still something you occasionally hear today, and for me always prompts the response "As opposed to the periphery?" But in that phrase, there were a number of valid challenges to the traditional mode of education, such as how to deal with abundant resources, numerous voices, and content of unknown origin, while operating in a networked world. The modern development of digital literacies might be seen as the descendant of the "guide on the side" idea.

In 2001 constructivism had become so popular in web-based learning that Oliver (2000) argued that "the theories of learning that hold the greatest sway today are those based on constructivist principles" (p. 18). And it did seem that just about every conference paper at the time opened with a piece on "student-centred" learning and their constructivist approach. In reality, this often equated to little more than saying,

"We gave them a forum." And sometimes it could be an excuse for poor design, a reason for the educator to absent themselves from creating content, because in constructivism everyone had to construct their own interpretation. Mayer (2004) suggested that such discovery-based approaches are less effective than guided ones, arguing that the "debate about discovery has been replayed many times in education but each time, the evidence has favoured a guided approach to learning" (p. 18). It is also an approach that doesn't apply equally across all disciplines; quantum physics, for example, is almost entirely theoretical and largely counter-intuitive, so bringing your own experience of quarks isn't going to help or expecting undergrad students to all have Einsteinian epiphanies is unlikely. It is probably also true to say that there was a sense of snobbery about it, as constructivism was the new way for the new technology and all the old-fashioned instructivist approaches were plain wrong.

There was a significant amount of research on effective online implementation. For example, Carr-Chellman and Duschatel (2000) proposed a series of components for an "ideal online course" after analyzing a range of successful ones. These components are summarized here:

A study guide: Online study guides must provide a level of detail that is sufficient to enable the learner to proceed without substantial further personal interaction or clarification from the instructor.

No online textbook: The ideal online course should generally not have the primary learning resources online.

Assignments: The course is centred on the set of student tasks (projects, assignments) that constitute the learning experiences that the students will engage in, either independently or collaboratively.

Examples online: The availability of prior student's work online.

Course communications: Emphasizing student-to-student interaction and using a range of communication methods that include asynchronous, synchronous, and email.

Interactive skill building: An approach that emphasizes
intellectual dialogue for all conceptual and advanced
intellectual skills development; dialogue that is developed
through the communication methods mentioned above.

From a modern perspective, this list holds up well as general principles
of course design and is an example of the type of research and approach
that was largely forgotten and then rediscovered with later ed tech
developments. Carr-Chellman and Duschatel (2000) emphasized that
their thinking was "aligned with current conceptions of constructivist
learning" (p. 237). However, not everyone was convinced of the possibility
of the new medium to implement effective learning. Bork and Britton
(1998) declared that the "web is not yet suitable for learning," and saw it
as primarily a support tool, concluding that they were concerned "with
situations in which the website is intended to be the primary delivery
method for learning, not when it is a supplement to learning delivered
mainly in other ways, such as through lecture" (p. 115). This judgment
may not have been overly harsh given the quality of many web-based
courses at the time, but it does highlight how a focus on current limitations can miss the broader, long-term implications.

This highlights that, even with the reservations described above,
constructivism was significant because it showed educators engaging
with technology in a meaningful, conceptual manner. The focus was not
simply on web technology but rather the possibilities it opened up for new
pedagogy. For example, Spiro, Feltovich, Feltovich, Jacobson, and Coulson
(1991) saw constructivism as a means to combine the possibility of hypertext and non-linear approaches to learning in "ill-structured domains":

More appropriate strategies for advanced learning and
instruction in ill-structured domains are in many ways
the opposite of what works best for introductory learning
and in more well-structured domains. For example,
compartmentalization of knowledge components is an effective
strategy in well-structured domains, but blocks effective
learning in more intertwined, ill-structured domains that
require high degrees of knowledge interconnectedness. (p. 29)

It also marked the first time many educators engaged with educational theory. This may sound surprising, but lecturers rarely undertook any formal education training at the time; it was usually a progression from researching a PhD into lecturing, with little consideration on models of teaching. The lecture was such a default assumption for university education that it almost didn't need training to implement but was simply built on one's own experience (good and bad). It took technology to cause that reflection on practice. As we saw with CMC, one benefit of technology has been to prompt such reflection by making explicit many hitherto implicit assumptions. Research conducted on the impact of open educational resources (OER) in 2014 similarly revealed that one of the main benefits of OER is that they cause educators to reflect on their own teaching practice (de los Arcos, Farrow, Perryman, Pitt, & Weller, 2014).

The interest in constructivism can be seen as symptomatic of an increased exploration of new pedagogies or as renewed interest in existing ones. In examining the current physical space, Michael Wesch (2008), a professor of social anthropology who focuses on the impact of new media, asked students what a lecture hall "said" about learning; in essence, what were the signals perceived by students of the standard learning environment. This would have been true in 1997 also. Students listed the following:

- to learn is to acquire information;

- information is scarce and hard to find;

- trust authority for good information;

- authorized information is beyond discussion;

- obey the authority; and

- follow along.

These are somewhat at odds with what most educators regard as key components in learning, such as dialogue, reflection, critical analysis, and so on. They were also at odds with what many perceived as the prominent benefits of the new online world. This environment was characterized by democratization, informality, shared knowledge, social interaction, and learner-generated content. Constructivism, then, offered a means of framing the possibilities of this new environment. However, it is not a pedagogy in itself, and so alongside renewed interest in learning theory came the application of a number of specific pedagogies. These included the pedagogies that follow.

Resource-Based Learning

Resource-based learning (RBL) emphasizes the learner's interaction and selection with a range of resources, including human ones. Rakes (1996) summarized it as a process where "students learn from his or her own interaction with a wide range of learning resources rather than from class exposition" (p. 52). If one views the web primarily as a collection of numerous, accessible resources, then RBL was a natural contender for renewed interest. Greene and Land (2000) saw the web as a "resource-based learning environment," but noted that students often encountered difficulties with an RBL approach due to a lack of digital skills, disorientation, incomplete knowledge, and deficits in quality appraisal. Their response to these issues is to construct appropriate scaffolding for learners. Like any pedagogy, it can be applied poorly, but what the RBL approach, particularly in tertiary education, highlights is the access to a vast range of resources that learners now possess. This removal of the filter to knowledge, and the lowering of barriers to access, represents a fundamental shift in education — from the lecturer or textbook being the sole arbiter of knowledge to an environment which is typified by abundance. Although there has been much progress in recognizing this, for example, in developing digital literacies, this shift and its implications is one that higher education is still struggling to accommodate.

Problem-Based Learning

Barrows and Tamblyn (1980) summarized problem-based learning (PBL) as "the learning that results from the process of working toward the understanding or resolution of a problem. The problem is encountered first in the learning process" (p. 1). This emphasizes that it is the presentation of an ill-structured, or open-ended, problem that frames the subsequent learning experience for students. They may work individually, or often in small collaborative groups, to reach a solution, drawing on a range of resources. The types of problems used are often those where there is not a single definite answer, and so it is suited to particular domains where this is common. The role of the teacher is one of facilitator, helping individuals or groups to overcome obstacles, providing useful resources and advice. In medical education, in particular, PBL has been well researched, and there has been some evidence that it is more effective than traditional methods (Vernon & Blake, 1993; Smits, Verbeek, & de Buisonjé, 2002). As with RBL (and perhaps in conjunction with it), PBL can be seen as shifting agency and activity to the learner, and thus needs careful support and scaffolding to work effectively, but it represents the type of learning many of us undertake on a daily basis using the Internet as our resource.

Communities of Practice

Lave and Wenger's (1991) book on situated learning and Wenger's (1998) influential book on communities of practice highlighted the social role in learning and the importance of apprenticeship. They proposed the concept of "legitimate peripheral participation," which not unlike the ZPD, proposes that participants move from the periphery in a community to its core by engaging in legitimate tasks. A very practical example of this is seen in open-source communities, where participants move from reading and occasionally commenting in forums to suggesting code fixes and taking on a range of functions, such as moderation and code commenting. Crowston and Howison (2005) proposed a hierarchical structure for open-source communities, consisting of the following layers:

- A centre of core developers, who contribute the majority of the code and oversee the overall project.

- In the next layer are the co-developers who submit patches, which are reviewed and checked in by core developers.

- Further out are the active users who do not contribute code but provide use-cases and bug-reports as well as testing new releases.

- Further out still are the many passive users of the software who do not contribute directly to the main forums.

Bacon and Dillon (2006) suggested that some of the practices seen in open-source communities can be adopted by higher education, particularly the process of peer-production and the situated method of teaching and learning. With its practical approach, self-direction, user-generated content, and social aspect, the communities of practice approach attracted much attention. As with the other pedagogies outlined here, it was not suitable for all domains; for example, what constitutes a "legitimate peripheral" task is easier to define in some domains than others, and the progress through these layers may be more readily mapped and achieved. The process of undertaking higher education itself can be viewed as one of entering a community of practice, moving from structured work to more independent research and analysis. This can provide a useful model for online courses, where becoming a member of the community itself is seen as a useful outcome.

This is a brief summary of some of the pedagogic approaches that the arrival of the Internet encouraged people to explore, and as such does not provide a detailed evaluation of each. What these approaches highlight is an interest in constructivism and related pedagogies as educators sought to match the nature of the environment of the web to education. The web and the Internet are now seen as unremarkable components of everyday life, and the online world has become more regulated and structured, so it could be argued that educators have ceased to ask these more fundamental questions regarding the different nature of that environment.

CHAPTER 05

1998

Wikis

Perhaps more than any other technology, wikis embody the spirit of optimism and philosophy of the open web. The wiki — a web page that could be jointly edited by anyone — was a significant shift in how users related to the Internet. The web democratized publishing, and the wiki made the process a collaborative, shared enterprise. In 1998 wikis were just breaking through in education. Ward Cunningham is credited with inventing them (and the term) in 1994, as a means for software developers to easily collaborate and communicate. Wikis had their own markup language, which made them rather technical to use, although later implementations such as Wikispaces made the process easier. Crucially they were based in the web browser, rather than any specialist software, again illustrating the point that universality is generally the victor in adoption.

Wikis encapsulated the promise of a dynamic, shared, and respectful space, in some respects echoing the collaborative knowledge construction set out in Vannevar Bush's (1945) original vision of "the memex," and culturally representing the San Francisco, hippie-based philosophy of early web communities such as the WELL (www.well.com) — after all, they were named after the Hawaiian word for *quick*. Accountability and transparency are built into their operation, because users can track edits, roll back versions, and monitor contributions. This, combined with the ethos behind them, led to a wiki culture, character-ized by beliefs in knowledge as a public good, the power of collaborative activity, an aversion to commercial and proprietary solutions, and a commitment to a strict knowledge production process. However, wiki culture is not without its own issues; for instance, there is a distinct gender imbalance in contributors to Wikipedia, and as a result the types of topic deemed significant (e.g., Graells-Garrido, Lalmas, & Menczer, 2015; Hill & Shaw, 2013).

The potential of wikis for education was immediately obvious. Students could work collaboratively on a document, not limited by space or time. The possibilities for this were seized upon in a number of ways. For instance, Guzdial (1998) developed a version of Cunningham's original wiki to create the CoWeb, a simple-to-use wiki tool implemented across a range of courses. He identified several ways in which educators and students used CoWeb, which I'll go into here.

INFORMATION SOURCE

A primary use of CoWeb was simply as a course website since it was easier to publish with at the time than many other methods. This barrier to publication and participation is still relevant; for instance, Brian Lamb, Alan Levine, and others have worked more recently on the idea of SPLOT, which stands variously for Smallest/Simplest, Possible/Portable, Open/Online, Learning/Living, Tool/Technology. Their argument is that publishing in the open web is powerful, but too many open web tools (for example, blogs) are seen as technical and specialist. The aim is to create simple tools, for instance using a form, that reduce the barrier to such publication. The SPLOT developers state two key principles: "Make it as easy as possible to post activity to the open web in an appealing and accessible way and allow users to do so without creating accounts or providing any required personal information" (http://splot.ca/about).

STUDENT INTRODUCTIONS

Educators often created a page where students could introduce themselves and hand in and review assignments. In some courses students would post their assignments when they were ready for grading, so students had an opportunity to see one another's work and even comment upon it.

COLLABORATIVE WRITING

Students were asked to do collaborative writing projects selecting from a range of topics.

ANCHORED DISCUSSION

An anchored discussion is one based around an initial topic or document. Examples might be students studying for a final exam by posting and critiquing answers to sample questions, or students asking questions about an anchor assignment. There were student-generated versions of these also; for example, discussions around difficult topics or assignments.

PROJECT CASE LIBRARY

Students were given a space to post their assignments after grading, thus creating a project case library for exemplary projects.

CROSS-CLASS PROJECTS

In one application of the CoWeb, the involvement of junior and senior students on the same course, who didn't get to meet otherwise, was the explicit goal.

HOT LIST

A frequently used and student-generated website was a "Hot List" of pages that were particularly useful or on which there were active discussions.

CHOOSE-YOUR-PATH ADVENTURE GAME

In one class students created an adventure game about one of their assignments, like a "Choose Your Own Adventure" book.

STUDENT INFORMATION PAGES

The CoWeb could be used as a place to post general information for others, relevant to the class or not.

Looking at this list now, I am struck by how radical and innovative many of these applications are. Social media, forums, and the LMS have replaced many of these functions — for instance, a student-run Facebook page may perform the role of student-anchored discussions — but the mixture here is an indication of all the changes possible when the control focus shifts. Far from seeming antiquated, a course implementing such approaches, regardless of the actual technology, would be seen as innovative now, and would no doubt face a number of institutional barriers to implementation.

It was, of course, the development of Wikipedia that saw the biggest success for wikis. Even now, when it is thoroughly embedded in our everyday lives, Wikipedia seems an unworkable idea. An online encyclopedia that anyone can edit should result in chaos. The disdain Wikipedia is held in by much of the traditional media is mainly because of the struggle to understand how such a process *does not* produce nonsense. It is the rigorous process of editing and focusing on verifiable knowledge that is perhaps Wikipedia's biggest contribution, not the actual technology it uses. For content to be retained in Wikipedia, it needs to meet three criteria: neutral point of view, verifiability, and no original research (https://en.wikipedia.org/wiki/Wikipedia:Editing_policy). What Wikipedia brought to the fore is twofold: 1. The remarkable scaling and distribution of knowledge on many diverse topics across the global population; 2. The unpredictable and dazzling array of topics that could be generated by removing the very formal constraints on inclusion in an encyclopedia.

The amazing thing about Wikipedia is not that it sometimes contains errors, but how few of these errors exist within its 5.5 million articles (counting only those in English). Back in 1998, the revolution in encyclopedia was Microsoft Encarta — multimedia and delivered on a CD-ROM, it made the expensive, dusty volumes of the Encyclopedia Britannica seem a thing of the past, almost overnight. And while Encarta certainly made encyclopedias more affordable, it was still essentially the same model — experts wrote the entries and the topics were determined by the publisher, so only the delivery format had changed. What Wikipedia demonstrated was that the format was only half the story, and probably the least interesting half. The real fundamental change was in the process of creating an encyclopedia that the new technology allowed.

Wikipedia is itself a useful tool in higher education. For example, there are online courses which encourage students to contribute and edit Wikipedia for topics relating to open educational resources (OER).

The course develops skills in the history and values of Wikipedia, as well as practical topics such as the Wiki markup code and how to construct a Wikipedia article (Wikipedia, 2017). This has the dual outcome of increasing the number of Wikipedia editors and adding to the overall number of entries on a particular topic (in this case OER, but the same would apply to any topic).

Far more common is the use of Wikipedia by students in the normal course of their studies. Head and Eisenberg (2010) reported that over half of the students they surveyed were frequent Wikipedia users, even if an instructor advised against it. When completing an assignment, students frequently consulted Wikipedia at some point during their course-related research. Their reasons for doing so were to obtain an overview of a topic and to help them get started with a subject and references.

While Wikipedia may be embedded in the education process and can now be seen as the default knowledge source globally, the use of wikis themselves has waned somewhat. This is undoubtedly partly a result of the rise of other technologies such as Google Docs for collaborative writing and social media for interaction. But it can also be seen as symptomatic of a change in attitude towards the role of the Internet in education. With Wikipedia's popularity, it might seem churlish to bemoan the fact that wikis failed to fulfill their potential. Nevertheless, that statement is probably true in terms of the use of wikis in teaching.

I saw Mark Guzdial present about CoWeb at a conference in 1998 and came back to the Open University as a new convert to the potential of wikis in education. But my enthusiasm ultimately did not materialize into the e-learning course, which we'll encounter in the next chapter, being presented in a wiki. Inevitably issues about control and quality won out. Similarly, one might ask why aren't MOOC delivered through wikis? That may not seem an obvious question, but wikis could be seen as a logical implementation platform. We will encounter MOOC later, but for now, consider that their initial aim was to utilize the benefits of large-scale student numbers in an informal learning context. Wikis might be interpreted as meeting these needs. It's not necessarily that wikis as a technology have not fully realized their potential, but rather, the approach to ed tech they represent — cooperative and participatory — has been replaced by a broadcast, commercial publisher model. This tension between the potential of the open, experimental approach to ed tech, personified by wikis, and the model that came to dominance in the ensuing decade, perhaps personified by the LMS, will be a key theme to explore in the following chapters.

CHAPTER 06

1999

E-Learning

In truth, 1999 is a bit late to situate e-learning; it had certainly been in use as a term for some time, but it was with the rise of the web, and the practice of adding the prefix "e" to everything, that saw it come to prominence. By 1999 the components of e-learning that we have seen in the preceding chapters were all in place. The web browser provided an easy to use, common interface; CMC tools and expertise had developed to the stage where online tuition was feasible in all disciplines; a range of pedagogies clustering around constructivism established a theoretical framework for implementation; and tools such as wikis fostered innovation and collaboration. At the turn of the century, e-learning was poised to become part of the mainstream of higher education. How this promise played out over the ensuing decade is one of the themes of the following chapters, and it is a tale of both success and of missed opportunity.

There was much angst about the implications of e-learning for higher education at the end of the 1990s. Noam (1995) predicted a "dim future" for universities, arguing that "the ultimate providers of an electronic curriculum will not be universities (they will merely break the ice) but rather commercial firms. Textbook publishers will establish sophisticated electronic courses taught by the most effective and prestigious lecturers" (p. 250). Given the rise of MOOC and the ventures into course offerings from publishers such as Pearson, this prediction now, in 2019, seems quite prescient.

In a series of articles under the heading "Digital Diploma Mills," Noble (1998) set out a number of objections to e-learning. Noble saw technology as a vehicle for the commercialization of higher education, and the undermining of the autonomy of academics:

> What is driving this headlong rush to implement new
> technology with so little regard for deliberation of the
> pedagogical and economic costs and at the risk of student
> and faculty alienation and opposition? A short answer might
> be the fear of getting left behind, the incessant pressures
> of "progress". But there is more to it. For the universities
> are not simply undergoing a technological transformation.
> Beneath that change, and camouflaged by it, lies another: the
> commercialization of higher education. For here as elsewhere
> technology is but a vehicle and a disarming disguise. (p. 356)

This could have been equally written in 2012 around the time of the rush to invest in MOOC. Thus, critical approaches to ed tech are not new, and just as the approaches tend to be reinvented, so do the concerns and issues. However, it was also true that much of the criticism of e-learning revealed a conceit regarding the superiority of face-to-face education over distance learning, and an assumption that face-to-face is the only valid form of education. For instance, Noble (1998) reported that "students want the genuine face-to-face education they paid for not a cyber–counterfeit" (p. 360). The focus of such criticisms was often on the life of the academic and overlooked the social function of distance, open, and flexible learning options. Notably, much of this criticism came from the United States, which is one of the few major countries not to have a national open university, and thus the attitude towards distance learning tends to be informed by low-quality correspondence education. This also drastically over-romanticized the quality of face-to-face education, prompting McDonald (2002) to ask, "Is as good as face-to-face as good as it gets?" (p. 10).

In a typical academic fashion, there was much debate around the definition of e-learning, and it was obligatory for one person at every conference to say in a rather self-satisfied manner "there's already an e in learning," suggesting that a new term was unnecessary. But it was a useful term, as it highlighted the profile of online components and the exploration of accompanying pedagogies. At the time, e-learning broadly covered any use of electronic media in learning, but gradually the interpretation came to focus more on online delivery. Online education, web-based instruction, networked learning—all of these terms were widely used to mean the same thing: education that was delivered in some respect through the Internet. This also saw the rise of a term that is still in use, that of blended learning. This term had various interpretations, with Driscoll (2002, p. 1) identifying four main forms: a blend of different forms of media or technology; of pedagogical approaches; of technology and face-to-face delivery; and, of technology with job tasks. Given the manner in which even students in primarily face-to-face settings employ Wikipedia and other online resources, it is difficult to imagine any higher education situation now which isn't blended to an extent, whether formally or informally. The blending of face-to-face provision with online delivery has been one area of significant growth, and it has allowed many "traditional" universities to offer flexible learning opportunities.

In 1999, I was part of a team that developed the Open University's (OU) first fully online undergraduate course—this one wasn't in a wiki (Weller, 2000). In keeping with the spirit of the times, a group of us were excited about the possibility of the Internet for education, and particularly for distance education. We wanted to explore what it would be like to deliver a course entirely online—no printed units, no accompanying material, video or audio cassettes, or face-to-face tutorials. This may sound like standard fare now, but it was radical in 1999, and frequently dismissed. It transpired that lots of people wanted to learn this way and had been waiting for an opportunity. The success of this course (some 12,000 students) almost overwhelmed the OU's systems and necessitated the invention of a whole new set of digital infrastructures and procedures to cope. More significantly, its success effectively ended the argument about e-learning and its potential for distance education at the OU, and after this good showing, it became an intrinsic part of the strategic direction.

This example is significant because it reveals that these students were keen to study this way and saw it as liberating, whereas most academics were reticent about its use, and frequently hid this reluctance behind concerns about students. It also illustrates one of the themes of this book, the historical amnesia prevalent in ed tech — online, large-scale courses weren't invented in 2012 with the arrival of MOOC. When *BBC News* breathlessly reports that the University of London is going to offer a degree online in 2018 (Coughlan, 2018), it illustrates that e-learning still has the ability to appear as something new.

One of the interesting aspects of e-learning was the consideration of costs. As we saw earlier, the idea of an infinite lecture hall gained much interest, because as Noam (1995) put it, "a curriculum, once created, could be offered electronically not just to hundreds of students nearby but to tens of thousands around the world" (p. 249). However, this idea, which simultaneously caused dismay amongst academics and delight amongst those who fund education, failed to fully appreciate the costs involved in education and, in particular, the difference between fixed and variable costs in course production and delivery. Traditional (pre-Internet) distance education models have high fixed costs but relatively low variable costs (Weller, 2004). The initial production cost is high, but then the price per student is relatively low. For instance, bespoke printed units or software simulations are costly to produce, taking time and requiring the input of a range of experts. However, once made, these components are relatively cheap to reproduce, so the costs do not increase greatly as the number of students increases. This model requires a significant number of students to reach a break-even point and is well-suited to large population courses which are presented over several years without much alteration. Variable costs, on the other hand, are those that increase linearly with the number of students. For example, the payment of part-time tutors does not achieve economies of scale — the larger the population, of a course, the greater the number of tutors required.

In an e-learning course, CMC will usually form a substantial component, particularly if, as we have seen, a constructivist approach is adopted, which promotes dialogue, collaboration, and student guidance.

This requires tutors and moderators to successfully implement the course. In the CMC chapter of his book, the research of e-learning expert Tony Bates (1995) revealed that the employment of these tutors and moderators becomes the main costs involved. Such a course will, therefore, entail a high variable cost component.

The arrival of e-learning, then, did not present a drastic reduction in the costs of higher education, although it did indicate a shift in the allocation of those resources in some cases. It was possible, although not always realized, to spend less in production, because digital resources were now replacing physical ones, and there was a greater potential for reuse. However, there is often a subsequent increase in expenditure during the presentation of a course, because of these increased support costs and a more rapid updating cycle. The low cost of e-learning myth keeps reoccurring, however, and was a motivation for much of the investment in MOOC. It came as no surprise to those with any history in e-learning that the large returns on investment envisaged did not come to pass.

E-learning set the framework for the next decade of ed tech. This period might be seen as the golden age of e-learning in some respects, as it was now in a position to move from the nascent, experimental stage, into mainstream, large-scale adoption.

CHAPTER 07

2000

Learning Objects

The discussion on costs in the preceding chapter leads directly into one of the motivations for the focus of this chapter, namely learning objects (LO). As e-learning gained wider adoption, a number of new approaches to content development were explored, often derived from computer science, with one such approach being the concept of LO. The concept is borrowed from software development, where the object-oriented programming approach defined software in terms of objects, which contain data, attributes, and methods. Programs are constructed by assembling objects and specifying how they communicate with each other. This had demonstrated the benefits of reusable, clearly defined pieces of functional code that could be implemented across multiple programs; for example, a shopping cart. This was both cost effective, in that programs could be assembled from existing units, and result in improved quality, since each program relied on proven functioning objects instead of inventing their own.

Learning objects seemed like a logical step in applying this model to e-learning. Prominent ed tech blogger Stephen Downes (2001) put forward the case for an object-based approach:

There are thousands of colleges and universities, each of which teaches, for example, a course in introductory trigonometry. Each such trigonometry course in each of these institutions describes, for example, the sine wave function. Moreover, because the properties of sine wave functions remain constant from institution to institution, we can assume that each institution's description of sine wave functions is more or less the same as other institutions. What we have, then, are thousands of similar descriptions of sine wave functions.... Now for the premise: the world does not need thousands of similar descriptions of sine wave functions available online. Rather, what the world needs is one, or maybe a dozen at most, descriptions of sine wave functions available online. The reasons are manifest. If some educational content, such as a description of sine wave functions, is available online, then it is available worldwide. (p. 1)

This made a lot of sense then, and it still makes a lot of sense today. Learning objects (LO) were potentially beneficial for learners, educators, learning platform providers, commercial companies, and publishers, so they generated a good deal of interest. Defining them would become a contentious issue, but a working definition from Mason and Rehak (2003) was "a digitized entity which can be used, reused or referenced during technology supported learning" (p. 21). A lot of work accompanied the LO gold rush: standards were developed to make them reusable, platforms were built to deploy them, content was produced in their style, and papers were written about them. But they never really gained widespread adoption despite the compelling rationale for their existence, which Downes (2001) and others set out. The failure to make them a reality is perhaps instructive for all ed tech proponents, so it is worth considering the issues that prevented their success, as avoiding these may be useful for adoption of other technologies. Here is a list of some of the main problems that bedevilled their implementation.

Overengineering

In the next chapter we will look at e-learning standards in detail, but for LO to work like software objects, they needed to be tightly standardized. This version of the LO dream went beyond Downes's (2001) sine wave simulation and had as its vision courses that were automatically assembled on the fly from a pool of LO for a personalized, just-in-time learning experience. The common metaphor was that LO would be like Lego bricks, which came in standard sizes and could be easily assembled into different structures. For this to be a reality, LO needed to be machine-friendly in terms of metadata, format, and structure. The result was that they became cumbersomely overengineered to the extent that no one would create them, and they lost any sense of being an interesting subject for educators to engage with.

Definition Debates

Related to the above, the ed tech field debated endlessly what an LO was. Every paper on the topic started with its own definition. It was exhausting. For some, it was defined as "anything that could be used in a learning context." This could be a photo, but it didn't even have to be digital — it could be a physical object. This definition ends up being so broad as to be meaningless. Other definitions were more general but specific to digital, and yet others had tight definitions around containing a specified learning outcome or meeting a certain standard. These definition debates highlighted two problems: Firstly, it emphasized the academic obsession with definitions to the point where most discussions about LO degenerated into two people endlessly debating the finer points of their preferred interpretation, which became off-putting to most people who just wanted to use them. Secondly, the more specific definitions helped determine what an LO was but ended up excluding too much, while the general ones were too broad. The definition problem hinted at a more fundamental issue with LO, which is next on the list.

The Reusability Paradox

Wiley (2002), who would go on to become one of the significant figures in the open education movement, got to the heart of the problem with LO, and particularly the vision of automated assembly with the reusability paradox. He argued that context is what makes learning meaningful for people, so the more context an LO has, the more useful it is for a learner. But while learners desire context, machines don't — for them to be reusable, LO should have as little context as possible, as this reduces the opportunities for their reuse. This leads to Wiley's paradox, which he summarizes as follows: "It turns out that reusability and pedagogical effectiveness are completely orthogonal to each other. Therefore, pedagogical effectiveness and potential for reuse are completely at odds with one another" (para. 3).

An Unfamiliarity Threshold

The idea was that LO would be like reusable code, but the concept of sharing chunks of code was already familiar to software developers before it was formalized in object-oriented programming. And even then, the concept was learned as part of a programming language. LO never achieved this for education, so the very idea seemed quite alien to many educators, and particularly in terms of digital content. It began to look less like an educational concept and more like a technical one. This meant that the approach was unlikely to reach the critical mass it needed in order to be useful.

The World Wasn't Ready

It can be argued, that like so many things in ed tech, it takes more than one attempt at a concept to be successful, each one building on the momentum of the previous. LO didn't take off, but OER did (to a greater extent anyway), and open textbooks more so, as we shall see in later chapters. The drive for reuse is still a current issue, and the provision of open licences makes this a more readily digestible concept now.

Education is Too Messy

This is perhaps an extension of Wiley's (2002) reusability paradox, but in coding, the boundaries of objects are fairly well delineated, but educational objects do not have such neat boundaries, particularly once you move beyond clearly defined concepts. To take Downes's (2001) example, a sine wave LO might be easily reusable, but very soon the way one person describes and illustrates even a shared concept will differ for PhD psychology students to first-year undergrad engineers, partly because you know what they want to do with it, and it helps to be able to link it into other concepts they are familiar with to scaffold understanding.

Reluctance From Educators

As well as being unfamiliar, there was also a reluctance from educators to share their carefully crafted material. This situation persists with OER — there simply isn't the same culture of sharing for teaching as exists for research. Existing reward structures are largely to blame; for example, citations of research papers are a key metric in evidencing significance, but having others download and reuse your teaching material is not as widely recognized (and is even actively discouraged in many instances).

They Didn't Fail

While LO repositories may not be competing with Google for web traffic, you could make the argument that they didn't fail. As mentioned above, an element of them morphed into OER, which was influential in the rise of MOOC, and a lot of the LO work fed into standardization around platforms, assessment, and content transfer. Publishers probably took the LO idea further than others and can access a multitude of subscribers who pay for e-learning content that can be redeployed in new contexts. The Blended Learning Consortium is a successful collection of further education colleges in the UK, which each pay a membership fee and in return have access to multimedia content for their courses.

The Consortium states that membership fees are "used to pay staff in member colleges to write, edit and develop learning objects" (http:// www.blc-fe.org). The Khan Academy provides simple videos explaining key concepts, which are widely used by teachers across the world. LO may be a successful failure after all.

Lamb (2018) was also involved in LO early on and has reflected on why the LO revolution failed to materialize. He suggested these three factors:

- People were willing to share, but only with some people. This meant the technology for sharing had to be complicated and restrictive.

- The tools we used to build learning resources were expensive and everybody seemed to be using different ones. So, we usually could not revise or customize work that was shared with us.

- Copyright appeared to be a problem everybody was terrified of and that nobody could solve. (para. 10)

Interestingly, learning objects combined with Web 2.0 and begat a short-lived interest in the concept of social objects a few years later. Social objects were defined (again definitions proved tricky) as something real or virtual that facilitates conversation, and thus social interaction. This emphasized the role of content in encouraging dialogue, but only if that content was good *social content*: this is not necessarily the same as what we usually think of as good academic content. For instance, content that may be imperfect is often good for encouraging others to participate, or content that is contentious may be better at stimulating debate. Wiley (2008) linked this concept back to LO stating that the function of good educational content is to encourage dialogue:

If your educational materials are not "social objects" — in other words, if you don't already understand that their main purpose is to bring people together so that social learning interactions can happen — why are you producing and sharing them?

A relevant follow-up question is, if you are not providing the functional space for these social learning interactions to happen in (or at least pointing to a space where they can), why are you producing and sharing them? This is the key question for all OER and OCW projects. (para. 6)

What this interest in social objects reveals is the interconnectedness of ideas in ed tech. From a consideration of e-learning costs and quality we derive the concept of reusable content, and this lays the foundations for developments in OER, which then combines with the interest in social networks generated by Web 2.0 to revisit the idea of learning objects as social objects, which in turn draws upon the constructivist pedagogies and role of dialogue we saw earlier. And though the LO revolution did not materialize, some of the core concepts that were embedded in the work on LO persisted, and people continued to work away at these, particularly in the areas of reuse and copyright. There are several successful ed tech applications today that have built on the remnants of LO development.

CHAPTER 08

2001

E-Learning Standards

This chapter brings together the two preceding ones on e-learning and learning objects (LO). By the turn of the millennium, e-learning was part of mainstream education provision. The Internet was no longer dismissed as a fad, and most universities were engaging in some form of e-learning, even if only as a support tool for campus students. After the initial flurry of activity, typified by something of a Wild West approach to creating your own website, there was a necessary, if slightly less enjoyable, rationalization of efforts. This meant developing platforms that could be easily set up to deliver e-learning across an institution (we'll come to the Learning Management System later), a more professional approach to the creation of e-learning content, the establishment of evidence on the effectiveness of e-learning — which often found there was no significant difference compared to traditional modes (Russell, 1999) — and initiatives to describe and share tools and content.

This maturing of e-learning gave rise to the development of several standards, particularly IMS (see https://www.imsglobal.org/ep/index. html). This body grew out of a 1995 EDUCAUSE project on Instructional Management Systems, hence IMS, although the organization would later drop the interpretation and retain the acronym. The aim was to address one of the problems Lamb (2018) identified in the previous chapter, namely that platforms and content developers all used different formats, and so it was difficult to take e-learning content from one context and deploy it elsewhere. This undermined the entire learning object ethos, and, at the time, many universities deployed more than one learning platform so they could not easily transfer content even within their own institution. The focus of IMS was then on interoperability in e-learning. Akin to having different electronic companies, each with their own types of plugs, the sector needed some form of standardization in order to progress.

IMS, therefore, set about developing standards to describe content, assessment, courses, and, more ambitiously, learning design. There are two main areas where interoperability is key: content and tools. By specifying standards for tools, it allows an educator to use a variety of web-based tools and plug these into the standard platform, and pass data between them. The Learning Tools Interoperability (LTI) standard of IMS attempted to realize this, and was successful to a degree, although the vision of a plug and play, service-oriented architecture that allowed someone to assemble a bespoke learning environment from a range of best-of-breed tools never quite materialized (we will look at this in chapter 18 on Personal Learning Environments). Interoperability of content was addressed by SCORM, which stands for Sharable Content Object Reference Model — note the presence of object language in the title. The aim of SCORM was to define a means of constructing content so that it could be deployed in any platform that was SCORM compliant. This went on to become an industry standard in specifying content and allowed content creators to produce content in one format, with the knowledge that it could be delivered in all the major platforms, rather than creating separate versions for each. Prior to the advent of SCORM, there was a good deal of overhead in switching content from one platform to another.

Perhaps the standard that causes many ed tech people to break out in a cold sweat is that of metadata, and particularly the Dublin Core. The Dublin Core Metadata Initiative (DCMI) was formed in the 1990s from a workshop series focusing on different metadata approaches. Metadata was used to describe a piece of content (such as a learning object) so that it could be discovered and deployed easily, and hopefully automatically.

The 2003 version of the Dublin Core Metadata Element set (DCMI, 2003) had the following fields (or "elements"):

Title: A name given to the resource.

Creator: An entity primarily responsible for making the content of the resource.

Subject: A topic of the content of the resource, expressed in keywords, key phrases, or classification codes.

Description: An account of the content of the resource, such as an abstract or table of contents.

Publisher: An entity, such as a person or an organization, responsible for making the resource available.

Contributor: An entity responsible for making changes to the content of the resource.

Date: A date of an event in the lifecycle (usually creation) of the resource.

Type: The nature or genre of the content of the resource.

Format: The physical or digital manifestation of the resource.

Identifier: An unambiguous reference to the resource within a given context.

Source: A reference to a resource from which the present resource is derived.

Language: The language of the intellectual content of the resource.

Relation: A reference to a related resource.

Coverage: The extent or scope of the content of the resource.

Rights: Information about rights held in and over the resource.

These 15 fields represent the basic set of vocabulary terms to describe any digital resource, such as videos, images, or web pages. It is not specific to learning content, and in order to be useful in an educational setting more fields are required to describe pedagogic attributes, such as learning outcomes, age range, difficulty, and so on. A further range of metadata standards developed based on describing learning objects. These were much more complex than the Dublin Core basic set; for instance, the set of the 2003 UK Learning Object Metadata Core (UK LOM Core, 2003) contained over 60 elements, including items such as meta-metadata, semantic density, and taxonomic path. Some elements were mandatory and others optional.

The reason that mention of metadata still induces wry chuckles from some in the ed tech field is that at the time it was largely human-derived. Even the basic set of the Dublin Core represents a significant overhead for every learning object a user might create. Erik Duval (2005), who did much of the early work on analytics, used to preach that "electronic forms must die," and much of the basic metadata generation shifted to machine-generated terms over subsequent years. But for the rich metadata required for learning objects, the human labour required was excessive. An educator would spend time crafting a useful activity and was then presented with pages of metadata to describe it, which often required more effort than the initial content. This was obviously not an approach that would scale. As well as simply being tiresome to complete, this level of description also became restrictive, in that it seemed to define exactly how the content should be used, and often that is unpredictable. The intentions behind the UK LOM Core and most e-learning standards were admirable, but they essentially offered a poor return on investment. In order to be useful, particularly with a vision of automatic assembly in mind, they needed to become increasingly complex. As this complexity increased, they became more specialized and required more effort to complete and work with, and thus fewer people used them. And if fewer people adopted them, then the benefit decreased in doing so, which meant they were caught in a cycle of diminishing return. In analyzing the problems with a later version of the LTI standard, Feldstein (2017) emphasized this return on investment:

One of the major implications that falls out of this circumstance is that organizations will not adopt the standard…unless they believe the benefits will outweigh the costs. If a specification is going to be broadly adopted, then it needs to be designed so that all the adopting parties will see direct benefit. Remember, every minute of developer time spent implementing a standard could have been spent developing a feature or fixing a bug instead. (para. 4)

As the standard became more complex, the costs of implementation began to outweigh the potential benefits. I had personal experience of this situation when I was involved with developing one of the pilot courses for the ill-fated UK eUniversity around 2002–2003 (Garrett, 2004). The UK eUniversity was a government initiative to develop a platform to deliver the best of UK higher education online across the world (much as FutureLearn would do later with MOOC). The university developed a whole new platform that was based on learning objects. Every object needed to have metadata based on the UK LOM Core entered by hand, and if a change was subsequently made to the learning object, for example, correcting a typo, then the nascent platform lost all the metadata and it had to be entered afresh. The long-term goal was that the university would create a repository across all courses, from all the different providers, by specifying all content as learning objects. However, this nirvana of a rich pool of easily discoverable content seemed a long way off when you were manually entering the same metadata for the third time, and indeed never materialized as the UK eUniversity faltered and later collapsed. The effort in creating those metadata fields did not equate to sufficient reward.

E-learning standards are an interesting case study in ed tech. They are much less prevalent in discussions today around e-learning. In some respects, that is a sign of their success — good standards retreat into the background and just help things work. But it's also the case that they failed in some of their ambition to have easily assembled, discoverable, plug-and-play content. The dream was that a learner would type in "course on climate change" and the program would automatically assemble the best content, with some automated assessment at the end.

This wildly underestimated the complexity of learning and overestimated the good quality of learning objects. So, while the standards community worked away effectively, it was surpassed in popular usage by the less specific, but more human approach to description and sharing that underlined the Web 2.0 explosion. We will look at this in chapter 13, but the success of folksonomies (user-created categories) over metadata and embedded code over SCORM is another example of the "good enough" principle. For anything complex, the formal standards of metadata and SCORM were required, but for popular usage, the Web 2.0 versions were adequate. For example, even those who worked on the UK LOM Core (Thomas, Campbell, Barker, & Hawksey, 2012) came to recognize its limitations and recommended the following:

> As a result of an increasing realisation that the UK LOM Core was not achieving the intended results, and partly in response to new approaches to resource description, such as folksonomies, informal tagging, and the use of platforms for resource sharing such as Flickr, YouTube and SlideShare, which did not support formal metadata schema, the decision was taken not to mandate the use of formal metadata schema for the UK OER Programme. (p. 38)

It is interesting to note that not only did some of the ideas from learning objects and standards later evolve into the work on open educational resources (OER) but many of the same personnel were involved; for example, Stephen Downes, David Wiley, Lorna Campbell, Brian Lamb, and Sheila MacNeill all contributed to this early field and then became significant voices in open education. This demonstrates that while some approaches do not achieve the success envisaged for them, the ideas and people involved develop the key ideas into more successful versions.

CHAPTER 09

2002

The Learning Management System

For 2002, the selection is the dominant and arguably most successful education technology, the Learning Management System (LMS), also known as the Virtual Learning Environment (VLE). All of the chapters in this book deserve books of their own, and in the case of the LMS, I actually *have* written a whole book on this topic (Weller, 2007c), so I am very aware that a brief chapter really can't do it justice.

The LMS provided an enterprise solution for e-learning for universities. It stands as the central e-learning technology, despite frequent proclamations of its demise. Prior to the LMS, e-learning provision was realized through a variety of tools, for instance: a bulletin board for communications, a content management system, and home-created web pages. The quality of these solutions was variable, often relying on the enthusiasm of one particular devotee. The combination of tools would also vary across any one university, with the medical school adopting a different set of tools to engineering, which varied again from humanities, and so on.

As e-learning became more central to university provision, both for blended learning and fully online offerings, this variety and reliability became more of an issue. The LMS offered a neat collection of the most popular tools, any one of which might not be as good as the best of the breed-specific tools but good enough (another example of the "good enough" principle). It allowed for a single, enterprise solution with associated training, technical support, and helpdesk features to be implemented across an institution. The advantage of this was that e-learning could progress more quickly across an entire institution if it was driven by strategy. However, over time this has come to seem something of a Faustian pact, with institutions finding themselves locked into contracts with vendors, and providers such as Blackboard attempting to file restrictive patents (Geist, 2006).

LMS uptake grew significantly over the first half of the decade, and by 2005 nearly all higher education institutions had deployed an LMS, but only 37% had a single one, with others operating multiple systems, with the intention to move to a single system (OECD, 2005, p 124). Commercial LMS providers included WebCT and Blackboard, and open-source solutions such as Moodle and Bodington were also available.

It has often been noted that when a new technology arrives, it tends to be used in old ways before its unique characteristics are recognized. So, for example, television was initially treated as "radio with pictures," before those working in television began to appreciate what could be done with the new medium. This is to be expected, as we search for new metaphors to understand the ways in which the new technologies can be used.

This approach applied to much of the early implementation of the LMS. In order to smooth the transition to the online environment, developers started by implementing a familiar model, the virtual classroom. In 2008, Conole, de Laat, Dillon, and Darby found that the LMS was often used as a place to dump notes and to replicate lectures rather than engage in the more experimental pedagogies we saw in chapter 4 on constructivism. In this approach, content analogous to lectures is laid out in a linear sequence with discussion forums comparable to tutorials linked to this. In the Bodington system, developers even went as far as to make this mapping explicit by making the interface a building that users had to navigate to a specific lecture room. This approach should have been an initial step to greater experimentation with online learning, but many institutions became "stuck" at this stage, and the LMS is a primary cause of this.

One of the issues with enterprise systems such as the LMS is that they require significant investment in terms of finance, expertise, time, and resources. They thus gain a momentum of their own. The reservation many educators have with the LMS is not necessarily the actual technology but rather the institutional "sediment" that builds up around it. Lanier (2002) refers to "software sedimentation," arguing that:

> Software sedimentation is a process whereby not only
> protocols, but the ideas embedded in them become mandatory.
> An example is the idea of the file.... Files are now taught to
> students as a fact of life as fundamental as a photon, even
> though they are a human invention. (p. 222)

For the LMS, this sediment can be seen in the structures that accrue around the system. Institutions invest significant amounts of money on technology and employ people who become experts in using that technology. Accompanying this, they develop administrative structures and processes that are couched in terms of the specific technology. There are roadmaps, guidelines, training programs, and reporting structures, which all help to embed the chosen tool. This creates a form of tool-focused solutionism — if an educator wants to achieve something in their course, and they ask their IT services department or educational support team for help, the answer will often be couched in terms of the question, "What is the Blackboard (or tool of your choice) way of implementing this?" Or, something to the effect of, "That isn't in our LMS road plan." This inevitably stifles innovation and is one of the common complaints against the LMS.

There are ways to combat this sedimentation process. For instance, it is possible to frame the processes in terms of the generic function rather than the specific technology, such as asking: what do we want the LMS to do? How do we make effective use of asynchronous communication to enhance student interaction? Can we design the use of tools in courses to improve retention? And also, to think beyond the existing technology, is it possible to have an ongoing experimentation program? Most of all, it is necessary to be aware of every institutional action that adds to the sediment and to be aware that the greater the accrual of such sediment, the more difficult it becomes to implement, or even contemplate, other solutions.

In the mid-2000s there was much interest in the idea of service-oriented architectures. Using a protocol called Simple Object Access Protocol (SOAP), which allowed the secure passing of data between tools, you could assemble a system from discrete services. This would ensure that the LMS would not be a collection of mediocre tools but a collection of the best-of-the-breed tools, curated to meet the needs of a specific institution (or department in that institution). While this occurred to an extent with the IMS LTI standard we saw in the previous chapter, it wasn't in the interest of LMS providers to pursue — and for many institutions they wanted an easy option — so installing Blackboard or Canvas, with its community and support, provided a ready solution to the LMS problem. This lock-in with specific tools has been one of the drivers for the sedimentation process.

In 2004, I became the first LMS director of the Open University (OU). Like many institutions, we had precisely the issue of diverse provision, with an in-house system for course content, the FirstClass conference system for computer-mediated communication (CMC), and a variety of other tools. Advocates of these technologies insisted they were better than any LMS, and the conclusion the team reached after extensive review was to adopt a service-oriented architecture. We argued that the particular demands of a large-scale university that offered distance education courses were not well met by an LMS that had a campus model inherent in its structure. However, the problem with a SOAP approach was that it required something to plug all these components into — a component motherboard, as it were. To realize this aim the OU opted for the open-source Moodle platform. This permitted enough customization while providing an agreed-upon infrastructure. The OU has been a great contributor to the Moodle community, and the adoption of an LMS dramatically accelerated our uptake of e-learning. But the SOAP approach never really took hold, partly because it wasn't as viable as it seemed, and partly because just maintaining and developing our version of Moodle became the main focus. The open-source approach allowed the development of tools within the Moodle framework, and today it is a sophisticated platform supporting nearly 200,000 learners. But, considering the costs invested in Moodle, the ability to move beyond it is hampered.

In 2007, I foolishly declared, "The VLE is dead" (Weller, 2007d), proclaiming that loosely coupled third-party tools represented the way forward. There was also a lively debate on "the VLE is dead" at the 2009 annual Association for Learning Technology (ALT) conference (Clay, 2009). The third-party tools I listed in my post (e.g., Wetpaint, Pageflakes, Jaiku) have largely all disappeared but the LMS is still going strong. Much like the lecture in higher education, reports of its demise, it seems, are always overstated. The Irish Learning Technology Associated published a special issue in 2018, a decade after my injudicious proclamation, which rightly highlighted the impact of the LMS, by analyzing responses to the VLEIreland survey, a cross-institutional survey of students in Irish higher education over a number of years. McAvinia and Risquez (2018) concluded that far from fading, the VLE has evolved:

> The newer VLEs and upgrades of the "traditional" brands offer features such as integrated social media tools and e-portfolios, and have lost the visual cues tying them to the classroom, such as book and blackboard imagery. The regeneration of the VLE is remarkable. (p. ii)

Indeed, the robustness of the LMS is one of its main attractions. For many in ed tech, the LMS is at the centre of their work, and it can often be an unglamorous role ensuring that a system works effectively for thousands of students, and the LMS doesn't get the credit it deserves in ed tech circles. Like universities themselves, part of the appeal of the LMS is its steadfast nature: experimenting with people's education (particularly when they pay for it themselves) is not something to be done lightly. But there is a balance to be struck between allowing freedom, innovation, and experimentation while maintaining the core functions. It may be a question of time—education moves slowly, and now that there is a level of stability with the LMS, more experimentation can happen around the fringes. It's not fashionable, but we should probably give the LMS a little respect, and a little love.

CHAPTER 10

2003

Blogs

Blogging developed alongside the more education-specific developments we have seen, and it was then co-opted into ed tech. In so doing,
it foreshadowed much of the Web 2.0 developments, with which it is
often bundled.

Blogging was a very obvious extension of the web. Once people
realized that anyone could publish on the web, they inevitably started
to publish diaries, journals, and regularly updated resources. Blogging
emerged from a simple version of online journals when syndication
became easy to implement. The advent of feeds, and particularly the
universal standard RSS (which had various definitions, but Really
Simple Syndication is probably the most appropriate), provided a means
for readers to subscribe to anyone's blog and receive regular updates.
This was as revolutionary as the liberation that web publishing initially
provided. If the web made everyone a publisher, then RSS made everyone a distributor.

People swiftly moved beyond journals. After all, what area wasn't
affected by the ability to create content freely, whenever you want, and
have it immediately distributed to your audience? Blogs and RSS-type
distribution were akin to giving everyone industrial powers. It's not
surprising that in 2019 we are still wrestling with the implications.

No other ed tech has continued to develop and solidify (as the proliferation of WordPress sites attests) and remain so full of potential. For almost every ed tech that comes along — e-portfolios, LMS, MOOC, OER, social media — there is a group, of which I would probably be a member, who propose that a blog version would be a better alternative.

Back in 2003, the use of blogs in education was just beginning and a fledgling community of educational bloggers was emerging. There was a particularly vibrant edu-blogging set in Canada, possibly as a result of large distances involved, and those interested in new technologies found others engaging in similar experimentation via blogs. This potential to expand the academic community through the informal use of blogs that were external to formal university systems was powerful and would be repeated later with social media. From the perspective of today, with ubiquitous social media, it is difficult to appreciate how liberating the advent of blogging was in higher education.

Blogging provided a new form of academic identity, and one that increasingly became as significant as the traditional identity that is formed through publications, teaching, and research grants. It came with its own cultural norms of informality, acknowledgement, experimentation, and support. Particularly in the early years, these norms were more significant to bloggers than disciplinary ones, to the extent that bloggers in different disciplines had more in common than bloggers and non-bloggers in the same discipline. This was known to produce tension; for instance, Costa (2013) has argued that "Higher education institutions are more likely to encourage conventional forms of publication than innovative approaches to research communication" (p. 171). She reported that academics with an online identity were adopting a "double gamers" strategy, whereby they slowly implemented cultural changes to practice while simultaneously engaging in traditional practice to remain relevant within their institutions (Costa, 2016). The online academic has had to negotiate two worlds simultaneously, which can have different modes of operation and value systems; as Costa (2016) put it, they end up playing two games. There is some effort to reconcile these modes with increasing recognition of the value of network identity in achieving scholarly goals, although most remuneration is still linked to traditional outputs, such as published articles and successful research grant income. This is in contrast with the online world that determines prestige through identities and attention (Stewart, 2015).

Blogs can be seen as the start of what would become a networked academic identity, which would become more prevalent with the Web 2.0 and social media boom. Veletsianos and Kimmons (2012) used the term Networked Participatory Scholarship (NPS) to encompass scholars' use of social networks to "pursue, share, reflect upon, critique, improve, validate, and further their scholarship" (p. 766). This has become a rich area for research as academics wrestle with some of the issues it raises. On the positive side, Stewart (2016) noted that establishing such an identity increases visibility for pre-tenure academics, and this can offer some protection in a climate of precarious academic labour: "Among the junior scholars and graduate students in the study, opportunities including media appearances, plenary addresses, and even academic positions were credited to longterm NPS investment and residency, and to resultant online visibility" (p. 76). Lupton (2014) reported that academics often use social media strategically to establish networks, share information, publicize and develop research, and provide and receive support. Similarly, a study of academic bloggers by Mewburn and Thompson (2013) found that they address academic work conditions and policy contexts, share information, and provide advice, operating a form of "gift economy."

However, on the negative side, the online world is one which Stewart (2016) notes can be characterized by "rampant misogyny, racism, and harassment" (p. 62). For all their potential to democratize the online space, such tools frequently reflect and reinforce existing prestige, with higher-ranked universities having more popular Twitter accounts (Jordan, 2017a), and professors generally developing larger networks than other positions in higher education (Jordan, 2017b).

Before this toxicity came to invade the online realm, there was a good deal of (perhaps naïve) optimism about the use of blogging in ed tech. At the time, there were many types of benefits that could be articulated for individuals who were blogging:

> The economics of reputation: Increasingly a reputation online came to be seen as a valuable commodity. It became

complementary to conventional scholarship, with an online reputation leading to an impact that was recognized traditionally, such as in keynote invitations, research collaborations, and increased citations for publications.

Engagement with a subject area: In many subject areas, the blogosphere was where much of the informed and detailed debate took place, and so engagement with it became part of normal academic activity.

Organizational status: Increasingly institutions came to recognize the value of academics with substantial online profiles.

Link to teaching: The type of content used in courses became increasingly diverse, and one model for including up-to-date information was to include blogs.

Public engagement: Blogs tended to have easier reading scores (Weller, 2007a), and could form part of an ecosystem around public engagement and dissemination of research. Blog posts, videos, and podcasts that accompanied formal publications could be used to explain research in more appropriate language for a wider audience.

Developing personal networks: Much as social media came to be used later, blogs established a means of building a network of contacts without the necessity of having to meet face-to-face.

Fast forward to the current Internet ecosystem and what blogs provide is a means of anchoring an online identity. It may be distributed across other media, such as YouTube, Twitter, Flickr, Instagram, and so on, but it provides a central hub for these. Increasingly, as data capitalism and the nefarious uses of our data have come to light, there has been a movement to "own your own domain." That is, to host your own tools on a web domain that is under your control, rather than simply using a third-party service. Watters (2016) has emphasized that this control and ownership of data is an educational imperative:

> When one controls — albeit temporarily — a domain name and a bit of server space, I contend, we act in resistance to an Internet culture and an Internet technology and an Internet business model in which we control little to nothing. We own little to nothing. (para. 4)

Blogs are not just a tool for educators, but increasingly for students also. Following on from the previous chapter, it is interesting to speculate what the current ed tech environment would look like if, in the early days, institutions had adopted blogging platforms as their LMS rather than the commercial products. This is not as far-fetched as it might seem — blogging tools such as WordPress can be constructed to deliver course content and have embedded discussions, and they are easily extendable with plug-ins for specific functions, resembling the sort of service-oriented architecture that was deemed desirable. Templated versions can be implemented for all students, so they have their own space to develop their identity, create assignments, and develop something akin to an e-portfolio (more on this later). In 2008, Jim Groom and others were promoting the idea of blogs as educational platforms:

> This model puts the power in the hands of the authors, which in turn provides the possibility for a far greater level of educational openness. These are platforms that provide many, if not all, of the features of more traditional LMSs, but exponentially move beyond them given the fact that they benefit from huge open source communities that are constantly enhancing the applications. (Groom, 2008a, para. 1)

What this comparison between the LMS and blogs reveals is more than a difference over software preferences; it reveals differing visions about the nature of ed tech. For many of the advocates of blogs, the vision of ed tech is one that embraces the open aspects of the original web.

To return to Watters' (2016) post on owning your own domain, she claims,

> The *rest* of ed-tech — the LMS, adaptive learning software, predictive analytics, surveillance tech through and through — is built on an ideology of data extraction, outsourcing, and neoliberalism. But the Web — and here I mean the Web as an ideal, to be sure, and less the Web in reality — has a stake in *public* scholarship and *public* infrastructure. (para. 26)

Groom and Lamb (2014) also bemoan this loss of the original vision of the web in how ed tech came to be deployed, and see the LMS as a key component in this:

> In the mid-1990s, college and university campuses were the epicenter of web culture. . . . This is a powerful and compelling narrative of higher education as a laboratory for the future. Two decades later . . . [h]igher education overall, perhaps concerned about the untamed territories of the open web and facing unquestionably profound challenges in extending its promise beyond the early adopters, cast its lot with a "system" that promised to "manage" this wild potential and peril. (p. 29)

However, contrary to this view is the fact that many learners are nervous about entering higher education, and particularly online environments. The LMS provides a structured, "safe" environment within which to learn. It is also designed to hook into existing university systems such as registration, assessment, and library systems. It is also the case that many educators feel uncomfortable in online environments and a more open approach might leave them floundering.

It is not necessarily a binary divide. For instance, there are commercial applications of blogs and of the open-source LMS, so it is more of a continuum. It represents something of a philosophical divide about how people view e-learning, and at its centre are degrees of control. Around 2009, I demonstrated blogs to some academics, and one of them commented that they were concerned that students could share links to content outside of the course — content that was not approved and thus might be misleading. This is, at its core, the challenge that the Internet poses for education — a move from a tightly controlled system to a less regulated and more open one. The blog versus the LMS debate is a representation of this, but it recurs in different forms (we shall see it again in different interpretations of MOOC, for instance). I started blogging in earnest after several abortive attempts in 2006, and six years later (Weller, 2012) I declared the commencement of blogging to be the best decision I made in my academic career. I would still hold to that in 2019.

CHAPTER 11

2004

Open Educational Resources

Now that the foundations of modern ed tech had been laid with the web, CMC, e-learning, and LMS, developments could take place that utilized this basis of awareness and technology. For 2004, the selection was open educational resources (OER), which represented one such development. In 2001, MIT announced its OpenCourseWare (OCW) initiative, which marked the real initiation of the OER movement, and in 2002 the first OER were released, and there was a move to engage with different forms of licences for educational content. The OER concept is a relatively, but perhaps deceptively, simple one, and has remained largely unchanged since the initial MIT project: creating educational content with an open licence so it could be accessed freely and adapted. UNESCO's (2012a) definition of an OER is "teaching, learning and research materials in any medium, digital or otherwise, that reside in the public domain or have been released under an open license that permits no-cost access, use, adaptation and redistribution by others with no or limited restrictions" (para. 1).

A key element to this definition is the stress on the licence that permits free use and repurposing. In order to satisfy the above definition, it is not enough simply to be free, it has to be reusable as well. There are different definitions of OER, but they are all quite similar. Unlike the definition debates that dogged learning objects, this fairly clear under-standing of the concept of OER has allowed it to develop quickly.

Other providers followed the example of MIT, by 2004 a new open education movement was developing, and it had moved beyond being just an experiment by a single institution. MIT's goal was to make all the learning materials used by their 1,800 courses available via the Internet, where the resources could be used and repurposed as desired by others, without charge. At the time, this announcement caused a good deal of debate, as it seemed to run counter to the conventional wisdom that "content is king" and to the online models that sought to develop paid subscription models. Simply giving content away — and not only giving it away but explicitly giving permission to others to alter it — was a model that many struggled to comprehend. It took an institution with the reputation of MIT to give some credence to this idea, but it should also be noted that MIT was operating from a position of extreme privilege. Giving away its content was unlikely to affect its student recruitment, and much of that content wasn't particularly useful outside of the MIT setting. But what it highlighted, contrary to many of the prophecies of doom we saw in chapter 6 on e-learning, was that there was more to an education than simply the content.

As we saw with learning objects earlier, inspiration had been taken from software coding on reusability of components. The software approach, and in particular open source software, also provided the roots for OER. The open-source movement can be seen as creating the context within which open education could flourish, partly by analogy, and partly by establishing a precedent, but there was also a very direct link in the figure of David Wiley. Influential in the initial interest around learning objects, he provided a bridge to OER through the development of licences. In 1998, he became interested in developing an open licence for educational content and contacted pioneers in the open-source world directly. Out of this came the open content licence, which he developed with publishers to establish the Open Publication Licence (OPL).

The OPL proved to be one of the key components, along with the Free Software Foundation's GNU General Public Licence, in develop-ing the Creative Commons licences, created by Lawrence Lessig and others. Creative Commons, which was founded in 2001, would go on to become the main licence that permitted reuse of materials and be widely adopted in the OER movement. In 2004, MIT would adopt Creative Commons, and others followed suit. These licences went on to become essential tools in the open education movement. The simple licences in Creative Commons allowed users to easily share resources and wasn't restricted to a software code. Key to the Creative Commons licences was the fact that they were permissive rather than restrictive. They allowed the user to do what the licence permitted without seeking permission. These licences became a very practical requirement for the OER movement to persuade institutions and individuals to release content openly, with the knowledge that their intellectual property was still maintained.

The OER movement has been something of a success story compared with some of the developments we cover in this book. There is a global OER movement, with at least three annual international conferences on the subject, and OER repositories in most major languages. Funding has been provided by foundations such as Hewlett and national bodies such as Jisc in the UK, and sustainable models that do not require external funding have begun to emerge, such as the Open University's OpenLearn project (Perryman, Law, & Law, 2013). The OER World Map (https://oerworldmap. org) lists nearly 1,000 institutions globally that are using OER and nearly 500 OER projects, while Creative Commons has estimated there are over one billion CC-licensed resources (Creative Commons, 2015).

This demonstrates a steady but not spectacular impact. When MOOC became headline news many in the OER field could only wonder why they attracted such attention when many of the same claims of newsworthiness could be made about OER. The potential of OER to become mainstream seems always just about to break. This "nearly there" phenomenon is a recurring theme in ed tech; for example, with artificial intelligence. Here are some areas on which OER could have a significant impact, and although the results are currently small scale, there is promise:

Student retention: Students in formal education at all levels often use OER to support their learning (Weller, de los Arcos, Farrow, Pitt, & McAndrew, 2015). Currently, this is done on their own initiative, but educators could make better use of promoting OER to offer a broader range of material.

Student recruitment: Higher education is increasingly expensive in many countries, so the idea of trying a subject for a year and then switching to a different course is not always feasible. In order to facilitate effective course choice (Simpson, 2004), the provision of OER is an ideal way for students to explore if the subject meets their interest.

Student costs: This is often couched in terms of open textbooks for formal learners, as we shall see later, but also more broadly in terms of allowing access to educational content that would otherwise be unaffordable for informal learners.

Pedagogic variety: Teachers, colleges, and universities all struggle with the issue of appropriate staff development, updating the curriculum, and incorporating technology. The use of OER by teachers led to teachers reflecting on their own practice (Weller et al., 2015) and resulted in them incorporating a greater variety of content and approaches in their teaching.

This desire for OER to "break through" may be misplaced, however. It is not the case that all educators need to be aware of OER for them to benefit. Seaman and Seaman (2017) reported that awareness of OER amongst U.S. educators was low (10% very aware and 20% aware) but was growing annually, and in 2018 awareness amongst U.S. educators had reached 50% (Seaman & Seaman, 2018). More broadly though, open education in general and OER specifically form a basis from which many other practices benefit, but often practitioners in those areas are unaware of OER explicitly. These secondary and tertiary levels of OER awareness likely represent a far greater audience than the primary one, so the sizes of these audiences can be viewed like the metaphorical iceberg, with increasing size in successive categories. OER users, then, can be classified as follows:

Primary OER users: This group is "OER aware" in that the term itself will have meaning for them, they are engaged with issues around open education, are aware of open licences, and are often advocates for OERs. This group has often been the focus of OER funding, conferences, and research, with the goal of growing the ranks of this audience.

Secondary OER users: This group may have some awareness of OER or open licences, but they have a pragmatic approach to them. OER are of secondary interest to their primary task, which is usually teaching. OER (and openness in general) can be seen as the substratum which allows some of their practice to flourish, but they are neither aware nor interested in open education itself; rather, they are interested in their own area and therefore OER are only of interest to the extent that they facilitate innovation or efficiency in this.

Tertiary OER users: This group will use OER amongst a mix of other media and often not differentiate between them. Awareness of licences is low and not a priority. OER are a "nice to have" option but not essential, and users are often largely consuming rather than creating and sharing.

Wiley (2009) raised the concept of "dark reuse," that is, whether reuse is happening in places that can't be observed, analogous to dark matter, or it simply isn't happening much at all. He poses the challenge to the OER movement about its aims:

> If our goal is catalyzing and facilitating significant amounts of reuse and adaptation of materials, we seem to be failing. . . . If our goal is to create fantastically popular websites loaded with free content visited by millions of people each month, who find great value in the content but never adapt or remix it, then we're doing fairly well. (paras. 4–5)

By considering these three levels of OER engagement, it is possible to see how both elements of Wiley's goals are realizable. The main focus of OER initiatives has often been the primary OER usage group. Here

OER are created, and there are OER advocacy missions. For example, Wild (2012) suggested a ladder of engagement for higher education staff that progresses from piecemeal to strategic to embedded use of OER. The implicit assumption is that one should encourage progression through these levels, that is, the route to success for OER is to increase the population of the primary OER group.

However, another approach may be to increase the penetration of OER into the secondary and tertiary levels. Awareness of OER repositories was very low amongst this group compared with resources such as the Khan Academy or TED. The focus for improving uptake for these groups, then, is to increase visibility, search engine optimization, and convenience of the resources themselves, without knowledge of open education. This might be realized by creating a trusted brand to compete with resources, such as TED.

OER has many strong advocates, and UNESCO (2012b), for example, phrased its promotion of OER in terms of supporting human rights to education. The OER movement is not without its critics, however, which stem from both practical and ideological bases. For example, Knox (2013) offered five criticisms of OER, including an under-theorization of "openness," privileging the institution, and a lack of focus on pedagogy. Almeida (2017) also addressed some of the political reservations, suggesting that OER reinforce a neoliberal perspective and devalue academic labour. For Kortemeyer (2013), it was the lack of significant change in higher education a decade after the launch of OER that was the issue.

Perhaps one of the strongest criticisms of OER is that they focus on content often to the exclusion of pedagogy and support structures. They are guilty of reinforcing a model based on the autodidact or on implementation through existing educational systems. For example, UNESCO (2018) updated its previous recommendations, but the focus remained on the provision of content. Given UNESCO's goal to "ensure inclusive and equitable quality education and promote lifelong opportunities for all," OER represent a necessary starting point, but they are not an end point, and it is the learner support that is associated with the content that is a necessary component of any OER system. For example,

UNESCO's "sustainability models for OER" are aimed at finding ways to fund the creation of OER but are silent on the need for models that will support learners. The sorts of learners one might envisage using OER in an equitable, lifelong learning scenario often lack the confidence or the necessary learning skills to make effective use of them. As we saw in chapter 6 on e-learning, supporting students is by far the most expensive part of the open education system — but it is also the most impactful. An OER solution that ignores how this support is delivered is not sufficiently dealing with the problem that OER set out to address.

However, even with these reservations, OER represents something of a success story in ed tech, growing into a global movement since its early days. It may not have transformed education in quite the way it was envisaged back in 2004, and many projects have floundered once funding ends, but through open textbooks and open educational practice (OEP), it continues to adapt and be relevant.

The general lessons from OER are that they largely succeeded where learning objects have failed because they tapped into existing practice (and open textbooks doubly so). The concept of sharing educational content with a licence, that doesn't restrict this distribution, is alien enough without all the accompanying standards and concepts associated with learning objects. The component parts needed to be in place: in this case, the digital platform, open licences, and the concept of sharing educational content.

CHAPTER 12

2005

Video

YouTube was founded in 2005, which already seems surprisingly recent, so much has it become a part of the cultural landscape. Former PayPal employees Jawed Karim, Steve Chen, and Chad Hurley realized there was no single place for video sharing and set up YouTube with venture capital funding. In just over a year it was acquired by Google, primarily to aid its search data.

As Internet access began to improve, and compression techniques along with it, the viability of streaming video reached a realistic point for many by 2005. YouTube and other video sharing services flourished, and the realization that you could make your own video and share it easily with others was the next step in the democratization of broadcast that had begun with the web. It transpired that people really wanted to share video. While we take it for granted now, these YouTube statistics (Omnicore, 2018) dwarf most conventional broadcasters:

- Total number of monthly active YouTube users: 1.9 billion

- Total number of daily active YouTube users: 30+ million

- Number of videos shared to date: 5+ billion

- Number of users creating content shared to date: 50 million

- Average viewing session: 40 minutes, up 50% year-over-year

- Number of videos watched per day: 5 billion

YouTube Demographics:

- 62% of YouTube users are male.

- 80% of YouTube users come from outside the U.S.

- Millennials prefer YouTube two to one over traditional television.

Perhaps the most interesting statistic in that list is the 50 million users creating content. Many of these are existing companies, such as the BBC, but that also represents a large number of content creators who were suddenly given a platform. While many of the videos created are low quality and of interest to only a handful of people, the format also released a wave of creativity and saw the rise of YouTube celebrities and millionaires. Perhaps more than any other site, YouTube came to define the idea of the "participatory culture." Jenkins, Purushotma, Weigel, Clinton, and Robison (2009) defined participatory culture as one where:

- there are relatively low barriers to artistic expression and civic engagement;

- there is strong support for creating and sharing what you create with others;

- there is some kind of informal mentorship whereby what is known by the most experienced gets passed along to newbies and novices;

- members feel that their contributions matter;

- members feel some degree of social connection with each other at least to the degree to which they care what other people think about what they have created. (p. 3)

This is relevant to education because the authors contend that the types of informal learning spaces people participate in on sites such as YouTube contrast with formal education in several ways. They posit the following differences in culture:

Formal Education	Informal Learning
Conservative	Experimental
Static	Innovative
Institutional structures	Provisional structures
Long-term changes	Respond to short-term needs
National, bureaucratic communities	Ad hoc and localized communities
Difficult to move in and out of	Easy to move between

This list reflects some of the optimism around new cultures prevalent at the time and is akin to much of the now-discredited digital natives' narrative in its sweeping generalizations. It also rather over-romanticizes the participatory culture and glosses over some of the issues that have become apparent, which we will explore in chapter 25. Nevertheless, it does highlight different types of cultural values, much like those mentioned in chapter 10 on blogging. If blogging raised those cultural tensions for educators, then video raised them for learners. Even if we accept the generalizations in this list, it raises several questions: To what extent does this matter? Should universities attempt to be more like the participatory culture, or should they be an antidote to it? The answer for Jenkins et al. (2009) is that the development of digital literacies acts as a bridge between these two cultures. Embedding digital literacies such as the evaluation of information sources, communication, and production of digital artifacts are a core component in much of education now; for example, the Welsh Digital Competence Framework (Learning Wales, 2018) raises this to a cross-curricula level, alongside numeracy and literacy.

The use of video within higher education has seen a substantial increase since 2005, particularly with the ease of embedding videos from sites such as YouTube. Before this, video was usually bespoke, commissioned, or purchased and was often prohibitively expensive.

What accompanied and reinforced the online video sharing revolution was a drastic reduction in the cost of production. It had become possible to produce a good quality video using mobile phones, and indeed some cinematic releases such as Steven Soderbergh's *Unsane* were filmed entirely on iPhones. Prior to the advent of smartphones, small and inexpensive digital video cameras such as the Flip camera (https://en.wikipedia.org/wiki/Flip_Video) and webcams meant video production became democratized and, as such, its position in education content was altered. This ease of production, combined with the availability of abundant, easily discoverable, and reusable video content on YouTube meant that producing a multimedia course was within reach of any educator. As we saw with learning objects, it was the success of the simple video explanations of key concepts that could be shared and embedded such as those from the Khan Academy, which realized some of the original vision of reusable content.

One development that has seen an increased interest in the use of video is the "flipped learning concept." This emerged from K–12 education, particularly in the U.S. where the Flipped Learning Network has promoted it as a model for teaching. The idea is to use the face-to-face classroom setting for more interactive, group-based work and discussion, while individual time at home is spent on learning concepts. This individual element is often realized through the provision of video. It has attracted criticism because it shifts the workload of learning to the home, so it requires a home environment where students are equipped with connected computers, and they must focus on watching videos and taking notes rather than reading books or writing essays. This privileges children who have stable home lives. In higher education, this may not be as strong a factor, since independent study always forms part of the study experience. However, there is debate as to whether this is an effective use of time. Rees (2014) went as far as to call it "depraved," stating, "You may [be] thinking that you're teaching more efficiently, but what you're really doing is putting the onus of learning entirely on the student" (para. 7). In a review of the use of flipped learning in higher education, O'Flaherty and Phillips (2015) found mixed results, including a number of positive student learning outcomes, a strong willingness for academics to engage in the flipped classroom, particularly for large first-year foundational STEM courses, and positive responses from students. However, they also reported that it required considerable time investment from educators, that in some subjects it was not popular with students, and that there were very few studies containing robust evidence demonstrating that flipped learning was more effective than conventional teaching methods. Similarly, Lundin, Rensfeldt, Hillman, Lantz-Andersson, and Peterson (2018) reviewed the literature and concluded that "it is difficult to identify when, under what circumstances and in what ways the flipped classroom approach might be relevant as a pedagogical choice" (p. 17). Like many approaches that acquire a catchy name, this can be both a blessing and a curse. Rethinking effective use of classroom time in a digital networked world, and the effective use of abundant resources, especially video, would seem to be a desirable pursuit in higher education. But following a prescriptive approach or failing to accommodate for the increased load on students and educators can be a result of pursuing an educational trend.

While the use of video in class, lecture, or course is common (Moran, Seaman, & Tinti-Kane, 2011), its use as an assessment format is still relatively limited. In some disciplines such as the arts it is more common, but, in 2019, it is still the case that text is the dominant communication form in education. New innovations in this area include courses like Digital Storytelling or ds106 (http://ds106.us) that are encouraging students to develop skills in creating GIFs and video in a range of inventive assignments. But many students will go through their education without being required to produce a video as a form of assessment, and we have not fully developed critical strictures for this medium that are as commonly accepted as they are for text. The use of student-generated video can lead to more engagement, increased personal involvement and satisfaction (Greene & Crespi, 2012). There is concern about students possessing the right skills, but with ease of production, this is less of an issue. Perhaps the issue is more that educators know what a good essay looks like, and how to assess it, but are less sure as to what constitutes a good video. Using student vloggers (video bloggers) to construct an image of campus life has been utilized by De Montfort University (DMU, 2018) and Queensland University of Technology (Delaney, Menzies, & Nelson, 2012) with successful results, but such projects are not linked directly to assessment.

For academics, the ability to be a broadcaster has significant appeal. This has inevitably led to a wealth of overlong talking-head video productions, which are rarely exciting, but nevertheless the cliché of "we are all broadcasters now" became true. It would take some time for the implications of this shift to become apparent, in terms of misinformation, trolls, and privacy, but the initial realization of this new-found ability was appealing. Researchers could now produce short, attractive video content to accompany a paper and thereby reach different audiences. It is also the case that the conference experience has been transformed by the ability to live stream easily to amplify an event so that it is possible to remotely participate, particularly in conjunction with Twitter discussions. While the creation of video is still done poorly more often than it is done well, and the comments section on YouTube is not a place to go for informed debate, it is the case that video has become a valuable additional tool for educators, learners, and researchers since its democratization in 2005.

CHAPTER 13

2006

Web 2.0

This chapter marks the culmination of the user-generated approach that started with the web and was further explored through blogs and video. Whether the Web 2.0 boom signified its zenith or nadir will depend on your perspective, but certainly after the Web 2.0 bust, a sense of reality and caution pervaded it.

The "2.0" suffix, much like the "e-" prefix in the late 1990s, began to be appended to everything: university 2.0, libraries 2.0, IT services 2.0, and so on. As such it quickly became both meaningless and annoying. But it is worth revisiting why it caused such excitement, since many of the issues it raised for education are still relevant. The labelling of 2.0 was to make it distinct from Web 1.0 sites (not that anyone had referred to it that way prior to Web 2.0), which were characterized by being static, with the user in a passive role, the contention was that Web 2.0 sites were characterized by social interaction, user-generated content, and sharing. This oversimplified the distinction between the two; for example, as we have seen, bulletin board systems had been encouraging this sort of interaction since the 1990s. However, there had been a significant shift in the ease and amount of sharing online, so Web 2.0 provided a practical term to group together these user-generated content services, including YouTube, Flickr, and blogs. As well as user-generated content, these sites used tools such as folksonomies (user-generated categories), easy means of sharing, such as embed codes and RSS, and open data tools that allowed mash-ups mixing one or more tools. It can also be viewed as more than just a useful term for a set of technologies; though, it seemed to capture a new mindset in our relation to the Internet.

The Web 2.0 term gained popularity from Tim O'Reilly's use of it in his influential 2005 essay, in which he set out the seven principles of Web 2.0. These included principles that were more targeted at developers but also some that had resonance for educators, including harnessing collective intelligence and realizing the significance of data. Around 2006 people began to consider the application of Web 2.0 in education, with Alexander (2006) being one of the first people to seriously explore the implications. For Alexander, it was the potential of techniques such as folksonomies that was significant (and, as we have seen, which overcame some of the problems with metadata). As he put it, "Popularly created metadata is a rarity. Yet as of February 2006, tag-centric Flickr hosts 100 million images" (para. 8). Similarly, social bookmarking through tools such as Delicious allowed those in education to share their valuable resources, find others with similar interests, and find new content. This dramatically aided students in their research by allowing them to gather valuable sets of resources in ways that would have previously been very labour intensive. He also highlighted the potential educational benefits of collaborative writing tools, and methods for searching and collating blogs and meta-services for combining different information sources. Looking at his list now, two things stand out. The first is that hardly any of the many tools he cited are still in operation, which suggests both that it is problematic to tie education into tools with short lifespans and that the ecosystem of tools is much diminished now. The second is that some of this potential has been addressed; for example, collaborative writing is now something of a commonplace practice through tools such as Google Docs, but much of it remains unfulfilled. Rather like the applications of wikis we saw earlier, it is not the case that we look back from our current vantage point and allow ourselves the complacency of having realized these innovative approaches and gone further. Rather, our pedagogical landscape looks more conservative if anything.

The Web 2.0 boom took off—followed by the inevitable bust, as it transpired that start-ups did require a feasible business plan after all. The collapse of the Web 2.0 boom and problems with some of the core concepts meant that by 2009 it was being declared dead (Techcrunch, 2009). Inherent in much of the Web 2.0 approach was the provision of a free service, which inevitably led to data being the key source for revenue, and gave rise to the oft-quoted line that "if you're not paying for it, then you're the product." As Web 2.0 morphed into the dominant social media platforms, the inherent issues around free speech and offensive behaviour came to the fore. In educational terms, this raises issues about duty of care for students, recognizing academic labour, and respecting marginalized groups. In the "anyone can make a Web 2.0 business" gold rush, the privileged male-developer culture of Silicon Valley was reinforced. The utopia of Web 2.0 turned out to be one with scant regard for employment laws, diversity, or social responsibility. A business approach that prioritized short-term acquisition of users (usually with the hope of being taken over by one of the large software companies) resulted in little emphasis on building long-term relationships with a community. Much of the Web 2.0 culture, then, was at odds with that of higher education, but to follow Alexander's (2006) example, it is worth revisiting some of the more general principles, stripped of the hyperbole, and analyzing what these more general principles hold for higher education.

There are significant cultural differences between the practices that characterize education and Web 2.0 communities. For example, the latter tend to be democratic, based on a bottom-up approach and socially oriented. By contrast, higher education operates largely as a hierarchically arranged system, places a high priority on quality assurance of the content that is realized through a largely top-down process of review and formal assessment, and focuses on the performance of the individual.

As with the participatory culture of video sharing, it is not necessarily the case that higher education *should* adopt these cultural values, but rather it is worth exploring whether there is a benefit in blending them into existing practice. There are three such aspects derived from the Web 2.0 approach that could have an impact on higher education:

unbundling, granularity, and quality. There are more possibilities, but these three illustrate the case for considering the more generic aspects of Web 2.0 beyond specific software.

Starting with the arrival of the first Internet boom, and then accelerated through Web 2.0, was the concept of unbundling. Web 2.0 and the Internet in general saw some of the bonds that held industries together weaken, with the consequence that their component parts became "unbundled" into separate web services. The idea of unbundling in higher education has attracted media attention and investment, although, in reality, the picture is mixed. Christensen, Horn, Caldera, and Soares (2011) have argued that the education system will inevitably be disrupted, because universities operate a "conflated business model," wherein several means of revenue generation function simultaneously, which leads to inefficiencies compared to providers who specialize in just one of them. Staton (2012) confidently predicted that "there is no polite way to say it: the private sector is coming for education, and American society should embrace it. Entrepreneurs are one of a set of forces that will challenge the existing system of higher education as we know it" (p. 1).

The Unbundled University project (Czerniewicz, 2019) set out to examine these types of claims around unbundling, the degree to which it was happening, and what its implications were for learners, educators, and universities. The researchers reported on possibilities for unbundling in all aspects of higher education and stated in their conclusion that "the situation is dynamic, in flux, and highly contested; it is being negotiated and renegotiated right now" (Czerniewicz, 2018, conclusion, para. 1). While unbundling poses a threat to the notion of universities and privileges certain types of learners, it also "can be part of the solution and can offer opportunities for reasonable and affordable access and education for all. Unbundling and rebundling are opening spaces, relationships, and opportunities that did not exist even five years ago. These processes can be harnessed and utilized for the good" (conclusion, para. 2).

The second aspect that Web 2.0 raises for education is a consideration of the granularity of education. Sharing services allowed smaller chunks of content to be distributed: clips from movies, individual songs rather than albums, photos out of context, and so on. Higher education, as conventionally interpreted, is typified by the undergraduate degree program. This takes three to four years of continuous study, comprises several modules, and has regular exam and assessment sessions, with students being assessed in terms of the knowledge they demonstrate of the taught modules. There are, of course, variations to each of these elements — study can occur at a distance, it can be part time, assessment can be within a portfolio and continuous, there can be breaks in study, and so on. But each of these adaptations is usually mapped on to the existing standard model. They represent modifications to it, not replacements. However, it may be that many of these assumptions are bound up in economic models that have their roots in the physical aspects of education. For example, if students must come to a physical campus, then it makes sense to bundle all their modules into a short time span to minimize inconvenience and to manage staff time.

These restrictions have moulded what we deem to constitute a higher education experience, but perhaps this packaging is merely a product of the physical format and administrative and financial structures have been built up around it. Even when courses have moved online, they have usually followed similar conventions in terms of length and assessment. Several initiatives attempt to tweak this granularity. We shall look at digital badges later, but means of assessing different sized chunks of learning, taken in different settings, can be seen as a means of attempting to make this granularity more flexible. For example, in New Zealand, the Quality Assurance Agency for higher education (NZQA, 2018) launched a scheme to recognize micro-credentials, which were identified as "smaller than qualifications and focus on skill development opportunities not currently catered for in the tertiary education system" (para. 2). The OERu, a global cooperative of universities offering open courses as OER, offer the first year of study free, and students can then transition into formal education (Czerniewicz, 2019). The Open University provides a course that allows students to bring learning acquired through OER on any subject and gain credit for it. What these and countless other endeavours illustrate is experimentation around the edges of what constitutes higher education.

The last consideration Web 2.0 raises for higher education is that of quality. Weinberger (2007) summarized the change that Web 2.0 brought as "filtering on the way out" rather than filtering on the way in. Higher education processes are nearly always based on filtering on the way in — the journal review process, creation of learning content, selection of research proposals, student admission. This is one method of maintaining quality, but the Web 2.0 approach of allowing anyone to publish, and then filtering through rating and relevance, may also have a place; for example, the open repository for physics publications, arXiv, has become the main site for such publications, and applies only a light filter.

These examples illustrate that while everyone (including myself) is now rather embarrassed by the enthusiasm they felt for Web 2.0 at the time, it contained within it some significant challenges and opportunities for higher education. While the rejection of much of Web 2.0 is understandable given the excessive hype that accompanied it, and the more we've come to appreciate the associated problems, there are still some core issues in terms of practice that education could benefit from, and in ed tech we need to find a way of oscillating less between extremes of acceptance and rejection and instead examine the more fundamental issues that can be explored.

CHAPTER 14

2007

Second Life and Virtual Worlds

Online virtual worlds and Second Life had been around for some time, with Linden Labs launching it in 2003, but 2007 marked a peak in interest, particularly in education. Second Life provided a virtual world, which people navigated through constructed avatars, interacting remotely with the avatars of other users. Unlike most virtual games of the time, it was an unbound universe, and users could create their own environments on "islands" they leased. People made real money by offering services within Second Life, for example, by allowing people to camp on their island, selling real estate, or making virtual goods for avatars. These were traded using Linden Dollars, which could be exchanged for "real" money via PayPal. Unlike games, there was no specified goal or end point, rather it provided a virtual, 3-D meeting space. This allowed universities to establish their own islands, and on these construct virtual campuses. There was a good deal of interest in its potential in 2007, with Jarmon, Traphagan, Mayrath, and Trivedi (2009) having estimated "that by 2012, 80% of active Internet users, including Fortune 500 enterprises, will have a 'Second Life' in some form of 3-D virtual world environment" and that "these virtual worlds are expected to have a large impact on teaching and learning in the very near future with pedagogical as well as brick-and-mortar implications" (p. 169).

The most common use was to deliver virtual lectures, but Baker, Wentz, and Woods (2009) reported a range of applications:

> Princeton University's SL campus hosts music performances in their virtual Alexander Hall. The SL campus of the University of North Carolina hosts a virtual health clinic. The University of Kentucky's SL site includes a library help center and an admissions and visitors center. Vassar College's site has a live video feed from the college's real-life quad. Faculty members can hold office hours in their virtual offices at the SL campus of Bowling Green State University. (p. 60)

The Second Life world could be integrated with the Learning Management System (LMS), particularly Moodle, to create a hybrid "Sloodle" system, which sought to utilize the strengths of both environments (Kemp & Livingstone, 2006).

> While virtual worlds had strong devotees, they didn't gain as much traction with students as envisaged, and most Second Life campuses are now deserted. Taking a tour of the deserted campuses in 2015 (which still cost $300 a month to maintain), Hogan (2015) reported:

> I didn't see a single other user during my tour. They are all truly abandoned.... They mostly are laid out in a way to evoke stereotypes of how college campuses should look, but mixed in is a streak of absurd choices, like classrooms in tree houses and pirate ships. (paras. 5–6)

This quote hints at one of the issues with Second Life — a lack of imagination. Campus scenes were often used to recreate an online lecture, for instance, a professor may have been represented by a seven-foot-tall purple cat, but it was a straightforward lecture, nonetheless. What this gained over simply live streaming a real lecture was not always apparent.

Virtual worlds such as Second Life had strong roots in role-playing games such as Dungeons & Dragons; though it didn't manage to shrug off its nerdy, role-playing origins, and many users felt an aversion to this legacy. Interestingly, these Dungeons & Dragons roots for ed tech kept recurring: when CMC was new, MUD (Multi-User Dungeons) and MOO (MUD, object-oriented) were amongst the first widespread uses. This was part of their appeal to many advocates, but for other learners these roots were off-putting.

The technology required good computer hardware with a high-end graphics card and high-speed (for the time) broadband connection to run effectively. Without these, and even with them sometimes, the rendering of the 3-D world could be slow, and glitches in navigation could arise. In addition, there was the problem of "vandalism" when users destroyed or defaced property, or "griefing" when disruptive users interfered with classes held in public spaces, although given the type of online abuse found in environments such as Twitter, accounts of paintballing a lecturer seem almost playful now. Accessibility was a significant issue with no screen reader support, so they were difficult, if not impossible, for visually impaired learners to use. The navigation also required continual manipulation, and so students with dexterity problems found the environment difficult to navigate and never left the Orientation Island. The problem Second Life demonstrates is what happens when the technology itself becomes the main focus and is the predominant topic of conversation. This can be interesting to explore if ed tech is the main interest, but the technical issues and the foregrounding of the different environment can get in the way if the subject is, say, calculus. What this raises is the question of scalability and applicability — does every ed tech have to be suitable for everyone? Does it matter if some people feel put off by it? Does this advantage some groups and disadvantage others? These are genuine questions, and Second Life is not alone in facing them.

We can perhaps think of social software as "horizontal" or "vertical." Horizontal ones are those that have a relatively low threshold to engagement — Instagram, Facebook, and Twitter are all examples of these. This has been key to their success — they can utilize the benefits of the network without requiring intensive contributions from all individuals. Even browsing adds to the value of the network. And then there is vertical social software, such as Second Life, which has a high threshold of participation, and users tend to spend a lot of time engaged with it. The consequence of this is that these tools need to meet a range of needs, hence Second Life could be used for work, socializing, shopping, and so on. But it means they are unlikely to acquire the broad appeal required for the mass networking seen in the horizontal social software tools.

One of the issues with Second Life was that it very strongly divided people into pro- and anti-camps, with little balanced perspective. As I mentioned at the end of the previous chapter, bouncing between extremes is not productive. This was partly a result of the monopoly that Second Life came to have in the space. Several alternatives existed, but Linden Labs had greater financial backing than most of these. The cost of maintaining islands increased, and the openness of the platform came into question. The Virtual Worlds Watch project, which followed UK academics' use of the range of virtual worlds, provides a useful archive for much of this history (Kirriemuir, n.d.).

However, with the success of virtual and augmented reality software such as Minecraft and Pokémon Go, with more robust technology and broadband, and with the widespread familiarity of avatars and gaming, virtual worlds for learning may be one of those technologies due for a comeback. Like many other applications of ed tech, the pattern may be one of overenthusiastic initial adoption, when it is applied as a universal tool, to a more selective and appropriate application now that enough general familiarity with the technology has been acquired. Second Life could have been useful in specific domains, where the virtual setting allowed users to do things they couldn't easily accomplish in the real world. It is this application that has continued to see development, for example, virtual worlds for medicine, chemistry, and engineering. The overenthusiasm for Second Life may seem naïve now, but I share some sympathy with Hogan (2015) who, after his tour of deserted campuses, concluded, "I actually like how most of these islands represent an attempt by education institutions to embrace the weirdness of the web. The current crop of education startups seem bland and antiseptic in comparison to these virtual worlds" (para. 14).

CHAPTER 15

2008

E-Portfolios

E-portfolios provide a digital means of gathering together a range of outputs, assessments, and resources for a student. Lorenzo and Ittelson (2005) defined them as "a digitized collection of artifacts, including demonstrations, resources, and accomplishments that represent an individual, group, community, organization, or institution" (p. 1). Beetham (2005) summarized them as a collection of digital resources:

- that provide evidence of an individual's progress and achievements;

- [are] drawn from both formal and informal learning activities;

- that are personally managed and owned by the learner;

- that can be used for review, reflection, and personal development planning;

- [and] that can be selectively accessed by other interested parties e.g. teachers, peers, assessors, awarding bodies, prospective employers. (p. 3)

Writing as early as 2002, Batson described e-portfolios as "too good to be true" (para. 7). In this, they are akin to learning objects, backed by clear logic and strong argument. They have not quite undergone the same fate as learning objects, and are heavily utilized in many institutions, but they have not led to the fundamental change in assessment practice that was once foretold.

The argument for e-portfolios is a compelling one — they provide a place to store all the evidence a learner gathers to exhibit learning, both formal and informal, in order to support lifelong learning and career development. It is an idea that has significant impact for education — instead of recognizing education at the level of qualification, such as a degree in a particular subject, it allows a more granular recognition of specific skills, linked to evidence. This means a student can demonstrate competencies such as teamwork, communication, and problem solving to potential employers in a more effective manner. Much of the potential of e-portfolios is aligned with some of the constructivist language around student-centred learning; for example, O'Keefe and Donnelly (2013) claimed that "students can take possession of their learning and view the assessment as a positive experience in which they are assessed for learning rather than the reverse" (p. 2).

The use of e-portfolios varies, with Chatham-Carpenter, Seawel, and Raschig (2010) having identified four main uses: reflective learning, employee marketing, program assessment, and showcasing professional standards. In a survey of 43 institutions using e-portfolios, they found that most were using them for more than one of these functions. Their use, however, was not always appreciated by students. Singh and Ritzhaupt (2006) found that many students did not perceive an e-portfolio as a valuable tool and identified a number of themes, which included a lack of support on how to use the system, a lack of understanding and buy-in from faculty members, high cost, an overly complex user interface, and a resistance to the expectation that all students should implement an e-portfolio as a graduation requirement. Students may sometimes resist new methods because they come with an overhead for adoption, but this resistance diminishes as support improves and the new methods become more commonplace. Some of the criticisms highlighted here are an indication of the problems that arise when implementing a new approach and technology in an area as sensitive as assessment.

One successful implementation of e-portfolios is the ePortfolio Ireland project (http://eportfoliohub.ie), a collaboration between institutions of higher education in Ireland that aims to establish a framework to encourage academic staff to incorporate e-portfolios into their courses. The evaluations examined the perception of e-portfolios from the perspective of students, faculty, and employers (ePortfolio Ireland, 2019). The results showed that nearly half of the students who took the survey were currently using the tool, and, of those, approximately half did so for their own use and half because they were directed to do so as part of their study. However, using e-portfolios for preparing for future employment and career development was not strongly reported, and 65% of respondents indicated that it took a lot of time to complete an e-portfolio and that this was a barrier to their use. From a faculty perspective, many reported positive outcomes, but very few staff used e-portfolios themselves.

The evaluations reported that 80% of employers indicated that they include e-portfolios as part of their recruitment. However, given that evidencing competencies to employers is seen as a key benefit of e-portfolios, their usage may not be affecting practice. Korn (2014) reported a similar finding, noting that "83% of respondents to a recent Association of American Colleges and Universities survey said an e-portfolio would be 'very' or 'fairly' useful in ensuring that job applicants have requisite knowledge and skills" (para. 6). However, actual practice by recruiters does not reflect this. Korn continued, "Hiring managers are skeptical that the Web portfolios will convey anything more than a résumé and interview" (para. 9). This makes sense — while employers will say that the extra information in an e-portfolio is useful, in practice, their having to work through many pieces of evidence submitted by many applicants in addition to their résumés and having to conduct interviews is probably too time consuming. It also indicates that entrenched practices such as CVs and interviews have their own momentum, and ed tech is not implemented in a social vacuum. The success of any technology lies in an alteration to accompanying practice more than the technology itself.

Although e-portfolios have achieved more success than learning objects, they have not become the standard form of assessment as proposed, although in some areas their uptake has gained significance. Some of their issues are akin to those that beleaguered learning objects. While not damning them, the following issues still hamper their adoption.

OVERCOMPLICATION

As was mentioned by many of the students in the studies quoted above, they found e-portfolios time consuming. E-portfolios need to link into institutional systems and meet different requirements. This has led to the development of an IMS standard (https://www.imsglobal.org/ep/index.html) that can export and move between institutions. In addition, e-portfolios require methods of locking down items so they can be assessed, a means of providing different views for different audiences, and so on. The result is software that can be overly complex for users.

INSTITUTIONAL, NOT USER FOCUSED

A related point is that the result is a solution that is sold or selected by institutions. An institution has a very different set of requirements than an individual. However, for e-portfolios to be successful as a lifelong learning tool, then it is the individuals that need to adopt them and be motivated to use them.

FOCUS ON THE TOOL, NOT THE SKILLS

The complex, institutionally focused tool that has been developed requires a good deal of training for students to use it, as was reported by many of the students in the studies referenced above. This support is crucial. The danger is that the e-portfolio becomes a tool used inside education only, focusing on a specific university's requirements, with little focus on the more general skills that are the main benefits of e-portfolios: sharing content, gathering and annotating resources, becoming part of a network, reflecting on work, commenting on other's achievements, and so on.

LACK OF OWNERSHIP

While the intention of e-portfolios is for students to take greater ownership of their assessment and learning, there is no clear evidence that students continue to use e-portfolios after graduation. This may be a result of the e-portfolios' institutional focus. Jim Groom (2008b) and others have proposed that blogs provide a better option for e-portfolios than most bespoke software, claiming they provide students "a space that they can share, interact in, take with them, and build upon as they move onwards and upwards with their lives" (para. 4). E-portfolios enable tagging and comments, offer an easy means of embedding content, can be exported to other systems, and can be linked into institutional systems. More significantly, though, they are based on the individual and, as we saw in chapter 10 on blogging, they form an ideal basis for developing an ongoing digital identity. While not definite, I would contend that it is likely that more students would persist with a blog they initiated during their formal study than with an e-portfolio. For instance, how many of your colleagues do you know who maintain an e-portfolio compared with those who maintain a blog?

Although e-portfolio tools remain pertinent for many subjects, particularly vocational ones, for many students owning their own domains and blogs remains a better route to establishing a lifelong digital identity. If we were to consider e-portfolios as an instantiation of a more general approach of rethinking assessment and recognition, and then reimagine courses and pedagogy that would utilize this, then we would have an interesting case study. The technology is only part of the story in terms of their adoption; users have well-articulated reasons for their usage, but in order for these to be realized, the accompanying culture in higher education and employment also needs to adapt. Such cultural change is a slow process, and as with metadata, the return on investment for such change needs to be worthwhile. E-portfolios are currently engaged with the task of establishing this case.

CHAPTER 16

2009

Twitter and Social Media

If the Learning Management System (LMS) represents the dominant educational technology, then Twitter is the behemoth of third-party tech that has been adopted in education. There's too much that can be said about Twitter to do the subject justice in a short chapter, and most people will have their own views on its role in education, but it would be remiss to leave it out of any historical account. Founded in 2006, Twitter had moved well beyond the tech-enthusiast bubble by 2009 but had yet to become the pervasive tool of today. Not long ago I passed a highway sign signalling some road work; the sign stated that updates could be searched by using the hashtag of the highway number. While this wouldn't just be on Twitter, the use of hashtags as the most effective way to convey public information indicated that, since 2009, Twitter has gone onto to become, like the highway network, part of the infrastructure. In this transformation, it has also become a tool for wreaking political mayhem, populated by trolls, bots, and the far right, where daily outrages and generally toxic behaviour have become the most significant aspect of its usage. Given this, it is difficult to recall the optimism that we once held for Twitter as well as for Facebook. In 2009, though, the ability to make global connections, to easily cross disciplines, and to engage in meaningful discussion — all before breakfast — was revolutionary.

There was also a democratizing effect: formal academic status was not significant since users were judged on the value of their contributions to the network. In educational terms, social media has done much to change the nature of the relationship between academics, students, and the institution. It remains a means of creating a valuable and rewarding network for scholars that brings real benefits. How, then, are we to resolve this quandary of benefit and damage? For some, the benefits are no longer significant enough and they have quit social media, while others have moved to other sites, such as Mastadon, in an attempt to create communities from scratch that conform to more acceptable norms. One way of approaching Twitter and related social media is to view them as paradoxes, where opposing outcomes are both simultaneously true. This approach at least allows users to avoid the extremes of wholesale acceptance or rejection and attempt to find strategies that can, as the song says, accentuate the positive.

Strategies to Offset the Paradoxes

What follows are examples of strategies that can offset the paradoxes.

DEMOCRATIZATION VERSUS MARGINALIZATION

Twitter can practically democratize the academic space; for instance, many of the conferences I have been to over the past two or three years have featured keynote speakers who are not eminent professors with a substantial list of publications but people who have established an online identity. They have interesting things to say online, have established powerful networks and communities and often give the best keynotes. Social media is a democratized, open space where traditional hierarchies don't carry as much value. But the opposite is also simultaneously true in that the same sort of groups who are marginalized in real life are marginalized online. Thus, the experience of a white, middle-aged male online will be very different to that of, say, a young woman of colour, and particularly if that woman is writing about subjects that attract trolls, such as feminism, climate change, technology, and so on. Therefore, when universities encourage academics to develop profiles in spaces such as Twitter, they may be reinforcing existing privilege because, for some groups, this will be a more positive experience than others. In addition, if a person has real-life influence and an existing network, these can be transferred to their online network, regardless of the content they produce, as seen with celebrities. The Matthew effect posits that power will accrue more to someone who already has power, and a version of this is in evidence in social media, where a person with 100K followers will gain more simply through their presence in the network, rather than through merit.

REWARD VERSUS PUNISHMENT

In *The Battle for Open* (Weller, 2014), I argued that open approaches, such as developing an online identity, establishing a community, and sharing resources and ideas through Twitter are an effective means to engage in many scholarly activities. For instance, papers that are tweeted and blogged tend to get cited more, and Twitter can be a very time efficient means of finding answers to specific queries. There is a high degree of reward, often in very practical terms for using Twitter. At the same time, however, there are significant risks, such as the type of online abuse mentioned previously, the loss of employment or the receipt of disciplinary action through an injudicious tweet, or being subject to formal complaints by a group taking offence to something controversial (a political statement, for example). Given the diversity of interests and passions involved on Twitter, this can arise more quickly than we might like to think.

INFORMED VERSUS MISINFORMED

Twitter can be a site for detailed and meaningful discussion. For example, the "Learning and Teaching in Higher Education" chat (https://lthechat. com/) is a successful weekly discussion around the hashtag #LTHEchat that is held every Wednesday, focuses on a different topic, with readings provided before the session. Similarly, the #PHDchat offers a regular discussion community for PhD researchers that "is a legitimate organizational structure situated around a core group of users that share resources, offer advice, and provide social and emotional support to each other" (Ford, Veletsianos, & Resta, 2014, p. 1). But we also know social media to be a space and culture that at times seems positively hostile to education and informed debate. Twitter conversations on many subjects often descend into little more than name-calling, but this is made worse by bots and trolls that specifically target keywords to spread misinformation.

SUPPORTIVE VERSUS DANGEROUS

Social media can be a genuinely welcoming, supportive place for academics. For instance, it creates a social bond with people such that attendance at conferences can be a less isolating experience. Often, fellow academics can help someone think through a tentative idea, offering suggestions. These connections are not inferior to the types of relationships that exist at work or friendships that exist in real life; they represent valuable, significant connections. But, as discussed already, it can also be an unpleasant space, and a positively dangerous one. Threats of physical violence, as well as sustained campaigns of abuse, have very significant impacts on the lives of those who suffer them. Universities, therefore, have a duty of care when they promote the use of social media to both staff and students.

SOCIAL MEDIA IN LEARNING

Educators, then, are faced with having to negotiate these complex para-doxes for both themselves and often on behalf of their students. There are no correct or single solutions to these puzzles, and appropriate strat-egies will depend on the individual, their context, the institution, and the motivation for adopting social media. On this latter point, there are several potential uses for social media in teaching and learning, which I will frame as a set of hypotheses. These are not guaranteed findings, but rather potential impacts for which there are some tentative reasons to propose them. By considering these possible impacts for social media, it is possible to determine the preferred use and, thus, the appropriate approach to take. By framing them as hypotheses it also stresses the need to evaluate the evidence that supports or contradicts them.

Social Media Increases Student Recruitment

The use of Twitter, Instagram, Facebook, and other social media by universities, students, and staff provides potential students with a good insight into student life and can act as an effective marketing tool (Constantinides & Zinck Stagno, 2011).

Social Media Increases Student Engagement

The use of social media helps blur boundaries between study and other aspects of life and provides an element that can be fitted in-between other activities in a way that more concentrated study activities cannot.

Social Media Increases Student Retention

Students who make social connections tend to stay with their studies (Astleitner, 2000). Conventionally, this is realized through societies and social functions. Social media provides a further means to enhance these bonds, and particularly for distance or part-time students.

Higher Education Has a Duty to Develop Expertise in Fake News and Misinformation

Mike Caulfield (2017a), who has done much of the work in exploring the impact of misinformation, has developed an online book and a wide range of activities to help develop these skills. They are likely to become increasingly significant as the quality of fake videos and sophisticated targeting improve. If 50% of 18- to 22-year-olds enter higher education, then developing these skills helps improve the cogency of the network overall.

What these hypotheses (and you can undoubtedly think of more) illustrate is that if we think of social media as a form of social infrastructure, then there are a variety of uses it can be put to, just as a network roadways can be used by different people with different goals. To extend this metaphor, the effectiveness of it to realize any of those goals will be dependent on many related factors. Using the roadways metaphor, it will depend on traffic conditions, other motorists, types of vehicles, fuel, and road networks. Whereas for social media, these factors will depend on expertise in using the network, engagement from others, the tone of the debate, and time.

ACHIEVING SUCH SOCIAL INFRASTRUCTURE IS NO ACCIDENT

Achieving infrastructure-like status is the primary goal for Internet giants such as Amazon, Apple, Google, Facebook, and Twitter. For instance, for a significant number of users, Facebook is viewed as the entirety of the Internet. Reporting on surveys in Indonesia and Nigeria,

Farrell (2015) stated that "large numbers of first-time adopters come online via Facebook's proprietary network, rather than via the open web" (para. 8). Similarly, Amazon has the goal of becoming the sole global retailer, and Google and Apple contest the battle to be the sole technology provider in people's lives, embedding their platforms and technology in their home, car, phone, and entertainment systems. Such a monopoly means that any provider who desires access to the markets they control must abide by the rules determined by these companies, whether that is in what type of content they permit, the data they have access to, or the revenue they require. In addition, they are unlikely to permit any company that acts as a competitor to flourish within their domain. So, while these corporations have inveigled their way to infrastructure status, we should remember that providers of *physical* infrastructure systems such as water, roads, and power have responsibilities and accountability placed upon them. This is relevant to ed tech, because it highlights the responsibility in mandating the use of such systems and thus increasing their infrastructure-like status and stresses the import-ance of developing a critical approach to technology in all subject areas.

Social Media and Research

Having looked at possible uses of social media in teaching and learn-ing, we can also undertake a similar exercise for research. If we view a typical research lifecycle, as shown in Figure 1, then for each of these, social media can be seen to offer alternatives or opportunities to enhance the phase. Taking each in turn we can examine some examples.

INITIAL IDEA

Social media can be a useful place to test out ideas and garner early feed-back. It can also be used to conduct lightweight pilot studies, surveys, and find possible collaborations.

SITUATE IN FIELD

Social media allows projects and people within a field to connect, to reach out to others who have done related work, and to develop an identity around a particular project.

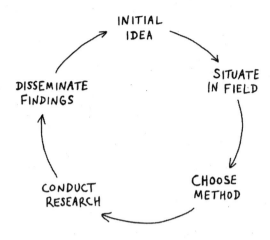

FIGURE 1. A typical research lifecycle.

CHOOSE METHOD

Social media allows for methods such as sentiment analysis, network analysis, subject recruitment, and survey dissemination, which can all form part of an overall methodology plan.

CONDUCT RESEARCH

During the research process, social media can be used to generate interest, disseminate early findings, and gather further collaborations and subjects.

DISSEMINATE FINDINGS

Disseminating work via social media brings greater visibility, citations, downloads, and linking through to the "open access citation advantage" (Eysenbach, 2006). But beyond this, there are other approaches to dissemination, including social media and video, to get across messages. Development of other outputs beyond the traditional papers, such as infographics, MOOC, and open tools, which are social media friendly can be produced to further dissemination.

What social media ultimately provides ed tech with is a set of tools and possibilities, but these are not without risks and issues. The clear distinction between professional and personal is deliberately blurred on social media. This can be beneficial, but it also leads to "context collapse." Marwick and boyd (2010) highlighted this issue:

> We present ourselves differently based on who we are talking to and where the conversation takes place — social contexts like a job interview, trivia night at a bar, or dinner with a partner differ in their norms and expectations ….The need for variable self-presentation is complicated by increasingly mainstream social media technologies that collapse multiple contexts and bring together commonly distinct audiences. (p. 1)

In other words, we communicate in social media with one audience in mind, but several different audiences might access that content. This is particularly true if you have a diverse audience, or if people use hashtags or search terms to find your tweets. This context collapse provides both an opportunity, for example in reaching new audiences for research dissemination, and a risk, for example trolls searching for terms to harass people. This is a reflection of what social media does for education as a whole — the context between the university and the rest of society is collapsed. That may be beneficial generally, but when it means conspiracy theorists arrive in a geology discussion to insist the world is flat, it raises problems that we are still incapable of solving. Twitter context collapse is akin to a black hole consuming all matter indiscriminately — cat pictures, sports discussion, political discussion, humorous memes, feminist movements, medical support communities, Nazi trolls, conspiracy theorists, and marketing — and in this academia is but one small part. Regaining and retaining an academic sense of identity and values, while deriving some of the benefits of context collapse, is the challenge that social media brings.

CHAPTER 17

2010

Connectivism

As we saw earlier, the initial enthusiasm for e-learning led to several pedagogies being resurrected or adopted to meet the new potential of the digital, networked context. Constructivism, problem-based learning, and resource-based learning all saw renewed interest as educators sought to harness the possibility of abundant content and networked learners.

By the late 2000s though, with the advent of greater connectivity, user-generated content, and social media, a number of educators began to explore the possibilities of education in a more networked, connected model that had these new developments as core assumptions. The theory of connectivism, as proposed by George Siemens and Stephen Downes in 2004–2005, could lay claim to being the first Internet-native learning theory. Siemens (2005) defined connectivism as "the integration of principles explored by chaos, network, and complexity and self-organization theories. Learning is a process that occurs within nebulous environments of shifting core elements — not entirely under the control of the individual" (para. 27).

Pinning down exactly what connectivism was could be difficult. Siemens (2005) stressed it was not a pedagogy, but rather could be viewed as a set of principles:

- Learning and knowledge rest in diversity of opinions.

- Learning is a process of connecting specialized nodes or information sources.

- Learning may reside in non-human appliances.

- Capacity to know more is more critical than what is currently known.

- Nurturing and maintaining connections is needed to facilitate continual learning.

- Ability to see connections between fields, ideas, and concepts is a core skill.

- Currency (accurate, up-to-date knowledge) is the intent of all connectivist learning activities.

- Decision-making is itself a learning process. Choosing what to learn and the meaning of incoming information is seen through the lens of a shifting reality. While there is a right answer now, it may be wrong tomorrow due to alterations in the information climate affecting the decision. (para. 30)

Key to the connectivist approach is the belief that knowledge is distributed in a network, and learning is a chaotic process. There is no single, correct set of objects of knowledge whereby education occurs through the transferral of knowledge from educator to learner, but rather knowledge and people are distributed, and it is the process of engagement with these that constitutes learning. It thus can be seen by Siemens (2005) as an attempt to embrace the nature of the Internet, which is characterized by its decentralization, multiple nodes, and changing nature. This is perhaps its most significant contribution — whereas other pedagogies sought to bring order to this chaos, connectivism takes this chaotic nature as a core principle and seeks approaches to navigate through it meaningfully.

What does connectivism look like in practice, then? Kop (2011) noted that it is characterized by four major types of activity: aggregation, in which learners access and curate a wide range of resources; relation, in which learners are encouraged to relate content to their earlier experiences; creation, in which learners are encouraged to create an artifact of their own, such as a blog post, using tools of their choosing; and *sharing*, in which learners share their work with others in the network. ·

Perhaps the most informative realization of connectivism was when Downes and Siemens developed their own courses, particularly the presentations of Connectivism and Connective Knowledge in 2008 and 2009 (known as CCK08 and CCK09), which were often attributed as being the first MOOC. These were open courses, in that anyone could study them at no financial cost, but also open in terms of content, direction, and technology. In CCK08 (Downes & Siemens, 2008), the content was distributed, so it was not located in one place but rather found anywhere online, with the "course" being constructed from connections and tools linking the content together. A key component was the use of a diversity of technologies, including Moodle, wiki, Elluminate (a synchronous communication tool), Twitter, Flickr, a central blog, and a daily mailing tool. Learners were encouraged to develop an online identity in blogging tools, such as Blogger or WordPress. This content was automatically aggregated by Downes and Siemens into a central collection. A newsletter was sent to distribute this aggregated content, as well as events and discussions, to learners every day. CCK09 (Downes & Siemens, 2009) followed a similar approach, but as the course guide noted, "What was most interesting about CCK09 is that the students from the previous year returned to the course again, and in many cases took over the teaching of the course" (p. 2).

From this brief description, it is apparent that this course would feel very different for learners than a conventional course. There is far less direction and structure, and there is a strong emphasis on creation and on making connections with each other. For some learners, this was a revelatory experience and they couldn't imagine studying any other way, but for others it was confusing. Kop (2011) identified three major challenges for learners in such a connectivist course:

- Self-directed learning: Learners have to be autonomous and confident to be able to learn independently, without the formal support structures, and to be comfortable in aggregating, relating, creating, and sharing activities.

- Presence: Connecting with other learners is a key aspect of connectivism, and so it requires learners to have a high degree of online presence. This is both time consuming and may not suit all learners.

- Critical literacies: In order to be able to work effectively in the distributed, technology based connectivist environment, learners need a range of competencies including technical ones, communication skills and the ability to critically assess content they find. (p. 21–23)

I implemented a similar approach on a MOOC some years later and experienced these reactions from students. Some found the approach liberating, others challenging, and some frustrating. One student commented to me that it felt like watching a party inside a house with your face pressed against the window outside. In a social-based course, being unable to find a way to participate, due to one of the challenges that Kop identified, can be an isolating experience.

What was most significant about connectivism was that it represented an attempt to rethink how learning is best realized by taking advantage of the new realities of a digital, networked, and open environment, as opposed to forcing technology into the service of existing practices. This approach has been surprisingly rare since. Dave Cormier, who is recognized as inventing the term "MOOC," and others have attempted rhizomatic learning that builds on the botanical metaphor of Deleuze and Guattari (1987). The rhizome plant has no defined centre and is constituted of a "number of semi-independent nodes, each of which is capable of growing and spreading on its own, bounded only by the limits of its habitat" (Cormier, 2008b, para. 3). This offers a metaphor of how knowledge is created in a networked context. As with connectivism, the best way to illustrate this is to consider an open course, Rhiz014, created by Cormier, which focused on exploring the concept of rhizomatic learning itself.

The mantra "the community is the curriculum" underlies much of the approach to this course, with the idea that participants were to generate a good deal of the content and structure it within a loose framework. The course covered six weeks and was framed around a question or challenge each week. After constructing a more traditional course format, Cormier (2014) reworked this to allow for a more participatory structure. He describes it thus:

> The topic I chose for week 1 mirrored the opening content
> I was going to suggest but with no readings offered. I gave
> the participants "Cheating as Learning" as a topic, a challenge
> to see the concept of cheating as a way of deconstructing
> learning, and a five-minute introductory video. (p. 109)

The result was that participants interpreted the question in different ways and had a range of discussions. Although the course technically ended after six weeks, it persisted as a community afterwards. As with the connectivist course, the conversations occurred across a range of tools.

Similar to connectivism, this socially oriented, less structured approach poses challenges for some learners. It again relies on a certain set of critical skills and the ability to navigate a complex space without direction. Mackness and Bell (2015) reported many positive reactions from the participants in Rhizo14, noting a sense of "a spirit of exploration, openness and experimentation" (p. 32). However, they also noted that some learners felt isolated. It is notable that with both the early connectivist and rhizomatic courses, the subject was the pedagogy itself. Thus, any frustrations in the learning process are valuable experiences in understanding how it works, and are, in essence, content related to the core topic. If the topic was something more distant, like statistics for example, then this overhead in negotiating the learning process might be excessive. Cormier (2008a) suggests that rhizomatic learning is particularly applicable to complex domains where there is no definite answer.

These limitations with connectivist and rhizomatic learning do not undermine them as valid approaches. After all, the conventional instructional model doesn't work well for many learners either, and it has its own set of challenges. As part of an undergraduate degree, we stress competencies such as critical thinking and collaborative working. Exposure to different learning approaches should also be a key component, as learning how to learn post-graduation is an equally important skill. Sanford, Merkel, and Madill (2011) explored how learning amongst video gamers takes a rhizomatic form, making such models more applicable to the learning a student engages with outside the formal education system, even though that system provides them with an opportunity to learn the relevant skills so they can make effective use of them afterwards.

Connectivism was an attempt to make the network nature of the current environment central in learning. I proposed a model that made abundant content the central aspect (Weller, 2011), suggesting that a "pedagogy of abundance" would have the following assumptions:

Content is free — not all content is free and not yet, but increasingly a free version can be located and so an assumption that this will be the default is more likely than one based on paywalls or micropayments.

Content is abundant — the quantity of content is now abundant as a result of easy publishing formats and digitization projects.

Content is varied — content is no longer predominantly text based.

Sharing is easy — through the use of tools such as social bookmarking, tagging, and linking the "cost" of sharing has largely disappeared.

Social based — this may not necessarily entail intensive interaction, filtering, and sharing as a by-product of individual actions constitutes a social approach to learning.

Connections are "light" — as with sharing, it is easy to make and preserve connections within a network since they do not necessitate one-to-one maintenance.

Organization is cheap — Shirky (2008) argues that the "cost" of organizing people has collapsed, which makes informal groupings more likely to occur and often more successful: "By making it easier for groups to self-assemble and for individuals to contribute to group effort without requiring formal management, these tools have radically altered the old limits on the size, sophistication, and scope of unsupervised effort" (p. 21).

Based on a generative system — Zittrain (2006) argues that unpredictability and freedom are essential characteristics of the Internet and the reasons why it has generated so many innovative developments. Any pedagogy would seek to harness some element of this generative capability.

User generated content — related to the above, the ease of content generation will see not only a greater variety of formats for content, but courses being updated and constructed from learner's own content.

There has been more recent exploration around the concept of "open pedagogy" (Wiley, 2013), particularly as it relates to open textbooks, which will be addressed in later in chapter 20.

In general, though, it feels that the sense of experimentation and exploration that connectivism represented has dried up. Perhaps this is a result, as with the earlier adoption of constructivism, of the possibilities now seeming mundane; it was only when they seemed novel that people noticed any difference to what had gone before. We have stopped noticing the possibilities of networked technology; for example, while connectivism provided the basis for MOOC, these became known as CMOOC, and the approach they eventually adopted in the so-called XMOOC was far removed from this and fairly conservative. Even if it's not connectivism per se, it is a missed opportunity to continually revisit the impetus to examine the learning possibilities that led to its formulation.

CHAPTER 18

2011

Personal Learning Environments

Personal Learning Environments (PLE) were an outcome of the prolifer-ation of services that suddenly became available following the Web 2.0 boom, combined with the thinking around distributed learning that we looked at in the previous chapter. Learners and educators began to gather a set of tools to realize a number of functions. The collection of these learning-support tools, both formally and informally, began to be referred to as a Personal Learning Environments or PLE. Educause (2009) defined them as "tools, communities, and services that constitute the individual educational platforms that learners use to direct their own learning and pursue educational goals" (p.1). They could be viewed as a useful term for what people were doing with the tools, a framework for educators in how to approach social media in education, or a tech-nical solution that sought to integrate tools. They can also be viewed as a reaction against Learning Management Systems (LMS), arising from some of the dissatisfaction with those tools we saw in chapter 9. Dabbagh and Kitsantas (2012) claimed that

> LMS have always been under the control of the institution, its faculty and administrators, leaving little room for learners to manage and maintain a learning space that facilitates their own learning activities as well as connections to peers and social networks across time and place. (p. 4)

PLE were seen as a means of allowing greater learner control and personalization, in keeping with the learner-centred approaches to education. Van Harmelan (2006) identified four motivations for their adoption:

Life-long learning — Allows users to have a system that persists beyond formal education and that also interfaces to institutional e-learning systems.

Beyond the LMS — A reaction to the perception that LMS do not offer the required flexibility or usability of many of the tools that constitute a PLE.

Pedagogy related — According to many of the pedagogic approaches being adopted, there was a strong emphasis on the learner's control of their environment.

Offline learning — Some learners needed to perform learning activities offline, without connectivity to a server, and a range of tools in a PLE could facilitate this.

Similarly, Attwell (2007) saw PLE as a response to changes in the nature of education, including an increased emphasis on lifelong learning, increased possibilities for informal learning, the development of new approaches to assessment and the recognition of learning such as e-portfolios, and the changing technological landscape.

PLEs were often visualized in terms of a spoke diagram (Leslie, 2012), showing the range of tools the individual used in an everyday learning context. In ed tech circles, the conversation turned to whether these tools could be somehow "glued" together in terms of data. Norman (2008) stated the central challenge as a question:

How can software provide what appears to be a centralized service, based on the decentralized and distributed publishings [sic] of the members of a group or community, and honour the flexible and dynamic nature of the various groups and communities to which a person belongs? (para. 1)

Instead of talking about one LMS provided to all students, the vision was how each learner could create their own particular blend of tools.

Wilson et al. (2007) set out a model for how this might be realized through an open application programming interface (API) and through standards such as Atom, FOAF (Friend-of-a-Friend), and RSS (Rich Site Summary, or Really Simple Syndication) for feeds. They contrast this type of learning environment with the conventional LMS on a number of dimensions, emphasizing that "the system should focus instead on coordinating connections between the user and a wide range of services offered by organizations and other individuals" (p. 31). This approach would go on to form the basis of the PLEX (Personal Learning Environment X) project (http://www.reload.ac.uk/plex), a prototype tool from the University of Bolton that allowed users to glue together different elements. The social network system Elgg also met many of the PLE requirements, providing users with tools such as blogging, podcast support, user profiles, content aggregation, community building tools, tagging, and so on. Sharma (2008) stated that "Elgg can also be set up to integrate with other popular web-based tools like blogs and wikis. It can also be expanded with plug-ins to provide a calendar, a wiki, or advertisement" (p. 13).

By 2014, the PLE had largely faded from conversation. As with other ed tech innovations that have a solid theoretical basis but fail to realize their potential, it is worth exploring the reasons for this. Here are some possible reasons why the PLE didn't gain mainstream adoption:

> The concept became absorbed, so it was seen as an extension of the LMS, or rather the LMS was just one other part of it. People don't differentiate between tools for different settings because the boundaries between personal and professional have been blurred.

> There was a consolidation in the market after the Web 2.0 bust, so most people settled on the same few tools: Twitter, YouTube, WordPress, Wikipedia, plus some other specific ones. One PLE began to look similar to any other PLE, which meant it was no longer personal. Just as with the early days of search engines, we no longer talk about whether you prefer Lycos or WebCrawler now, we just Google it.

It wasn't a useful term or approach. Some projects attempted to get data passed between LMS and PLE tools, or to set these up for people and, in the end, people just opted for tools they found useful and didn't feel the need to go further.

The overhead for learners was too high. For learners engaged in formal education, coping with the conceptual challenges of their particular field of study is difficult enough without requiring them to construct their own learning environment.

It was too complex. The appeal of an LMS is that it easily meets a demand and is geared towards the type of procurement process in place at most institutions. Implementing an enterprise version of a PLE that would not only integrate all of the third-party tools but link effectively with university registration, timetabling, and accreditation systems was too complex for too little gain.

It was likely a combination of all of these factors. Combined with this was increasing wariness about applications that shared data. Providing a uniform offering and technical support for learners was difficult when they were all using different tools. Ultimately, as with other developments we have seen, the return on investment from an individual or an institution was not significant enough, the benefits too abstract, and the immediate difficulties too obstructive. Looking at the motivations for the PLE interest, though, it marks a high point of educational technologists reflecting on the environment that technology creates and its implications for learning.

The use of the term PLE may have faded, but it has been replaced by a more people-focused version, with the term PLN (Personal Learning Network). As social media became ubiquitous, so the ability to develop a network of people that could enhance learning became a common practice. These needn't be people the individual interacts with; they can be those they follow on social media, read blogs by, listen to podcasts by, and so on, who aid learning. This really is personal, as it will often include people the individual knows locally, professionally, as well as those they encounter online. Although a PLN can include resources, it is a much more social, human-focused interpretation.

Further to the PLE and the PLN, personalized learning remains one of the dreams of ed tech, with learners enjoying a personalized curriculum, based on analytics. Indeed, personalization is often presented as an obvious, and unquestionable improvement, with Facebook founder Mark Zuckerberg, for example, announcing it as one of his key areas of philanthropy (Zuckerberg, 2017). While flexibility in a system and modification to meet the needs of different learners is undoubtedly desirable, complete personalization may not be as beneficial as is often believed. For example, Pane et al. (2017) report that students in personalized schools felt less positive about their school experience than those in traditional schools. Perhaps personalization erodes the sense of a cohort and shared experience with others, which is a significant part of the educational process. It may also place stress on students to feel like they need to direct their own learning as well as undertake it, when doing just one of those might be enough. Similarly, at the Open University of the Netherlands, Schlusmans, van den Munckhof, and Nielissen (2017) reported that their previously highly personal, flexible model, which involved a "start any time, take an exam any time" approach, was in fact, *too* flexible. It worked for highly independent learners, but since switching to a more structured approach there has been an improvement in retention, and this more tightly controlled model has allowed for more interactive pedagogy.

Personalization is a challenge for higher education, which the advent of networked technologies has brought to the fore. When students are accustomed to personalization in all aspects of their lives, from their Starbucks order to their music playlists in Spotify, then they may well expect the same in higher education. One of the technologies this book has not covered is the student portal, which can be seen as an attempt to provide this at a convenient, if superficial, level by allowing students to personalize what news and feeds they receive. Personalizing learning is more complex, however. It might be desirable to have a system that can automatically suggest OER to students if they are struggling, based on their preferences so far, but even in this case there is an argument for developing the skills to find OER by developing learning to learn skills. An automated system would remove this process. As the findings above suggest, fully personalized learning may not be as desirable as is often implied, because learning is often a social process and individualization can remove the opportunities for this.

CHAPTER 19

2012

Massive Open Online Courses

Inevitably, the selection for 2012 is massive open online courses, or MOOC, with *The New York Times* declaring it "the year of the MOOC" (Pappano, 2012). We have looked at the roots of MOOC in the explorations of connectivist approaches, but more broadly the MOOC phenomenon can be viewed as the combination of several preceding technologies: some of the open approach of OER, the application of video, and the revolutionary hype of Web 2.0. The MOOC were an idea waiting to happen, with several people experimenting with the idea of running courses in the open. For example, photographer Jonathan Worth (2015) had been running an open photography course, Phonar (short for photography and narrative), which combined his formal students with informal learners, and used open platforms for discussions. This was, for him, a means of exploring how photographers operate in the new digital economy. And, as we have seen, educators such as George Siemens, Stephen Downes, and others had experimented with course design to examine connected pedagogies. These had attracted attention within the ed tech community, but MOOC were still widely unknown outside of the field. However, once Stanford professor Sebastian Thrun's course on artificial intelligence attracted over 100,000 learners and almost as many headlines (Raith, 2011), the venture capitalist investment flooded in.

Perhaps more than any other ed tech in this book, MOOC generated a significant amount of media attention and hype; they are a case study still in the making. But now that the initial flurry of activity has died down, what can we say about MOOC?

First of all, their impact has been far less dramatic than has often been portrayed. Thrun famously declared that there will only be 10 global providers of higher education by 2022 (Leckart, 2012), and we can now assume that will not be the case. As I mentioned in the introduction, Shirky (2012) saw them as higher education's "Napster moment." Morgan (2016) argued that "MOOCs prove that universities can and should embrace online learning," and Godin (2016) proclaimed MOOC to be the "first generation of online learning." As well as overclaiming for the impact of MOOC, what many of these pieces have in common is a conflation of online learning with MOOCs. For instance, it didn't take the development of MOOC to show universities that they should embrace online learning, as Morgan contended. The examples in this book demonstrate that universities have been embracing online learning for at least 15 years. Such overblown claims constitute a semantic, historical, and conceptual land-grab.

A consequence of this conflation is that, if MOOC and the online courses are synonymous, then MOOC are seen as the *only* way of realizing online learning. For example, Lewin (2013) published his article entitled "After Setbacks, Online Courses Are Rethought" in *The New York Times* on the problems of Thrun's company, Udacity, and its approach to MOOC. In this narrative, MOOC failures become the failure of all online learning, and the future of MOOC becomes the future of all online learning.

Several problems began to emerge with MOOC after the initial enthusiasm, leading to the reining in of some of the ambitions. The key ones were:

Low Completion Rate—With around only 10% of registered students finishing the course, completion rates have been problematic for MOOC (Jordan, 2014).

Learner Demographics — Most successful MOOC learners were already well educated (Christensen et al., 2013), and this finding undermined claims of the MOOC democratizing learning.

Sustainability — We looked at e-learning costs in chapter 6. It came as no surprise then that, as MOOC became industrialized and required high-quality media outputs, its costs varied considerably, particularly when staff time, marketing, and support were factored in (Hollands & Tirthali, 2014). Finding sustainable business models that justified this expenditure has proven problematic.

These issues saw a change in tone around MOOC, with MOOC provider Coursera (2013) announcing that it was going to "explore MOOC based learning on campus." This proposed system resembled conventional blended learning, or e-learning, but on a new platform. Similarly, Georgia Tech announced it was offering a master's-level MOOC, which was not free (costing US$7,000), once again conflating online learning with MOOC, and Thrun's company Udacity "pivoted" to focus on corporate training.

Perhaps a telling example of the MOOC hype and reality was the San Jose State University pilot. In January 2013, the university partnered with Udacity to offer a blended version of MOOC augmented by on-campus instruction. The intention was to offer large-scale, inexpensive education. It was launched with much fanfare, with Ferenstein (2013) claiming that it was "a move that spells the end of higher education as we know it." He confidently predicted the pilot would succeed and expand to more universities. Instead, by December 2013, it was effectively finished "after a year of disappointing results and growing dismay among faculty members" (Straumsheim, 2013). This was portrayed as a failure of online education, but it demonstrated once again that support is the key element in provision, and that it cannot be provided cheaply.

What these examples illustrated was that MOOC providers were becoming platform companies to deliver e-learning within traditional education systems. It may have been cheaper than existing programs, but it was essentially the same model. Caulfield (2013a) suggested that commercial MOOC providers were never really interested in being free providers of education — they always wanted to become courseware providers to the education market. As he put it: "We now understand the endgame here. We now get the business model. The idea is not 'send your students to us!' The idea is to become yet another online vendor of services to higher ed" (para. 4). This is not necessarily a negative venture; a commercial e-learning provider could be helpful, and cheaper course options could benefit learners. But the arrival of new providers of LMS or e-learning content certainly doesn't warrant the coverage it received at the time.

Aside from all the hyperbole, what practical applications of the MOOC emerged? The most obvious one is that millions of people signed up for them and found them an enjoyable and useful learning experience. For example, Farrow, Ward, Klekociuk, and Vickers (2017) reported on over 11,000 participants in a MOOC on understanding dementia. As educators, the rise of such courses and increased knowledge has to be seen as a positive outcome. There are also examples of their use in formal education to expand the curriculum; for example, the Delft University of Technology offers a "Virtual Exchange Programme," whereby its campus-based students can take MOOC with other accredited providers and receive credit at Delft (Pickard, 2018). FutureLearn offers a program with the Open University and the University of Leeds, whereby learners' gain credit for studying in MOOC and transfer these into the university to count towards a degree (Coughlan, 2016). While such models will not appeal to everyone, they do allow increased flexibility in the higher education offering.

MOOC also raised the profile of ed tech, and open practice in particular. Even if MOOC themselves are only open in terms of enrolment and not in terms of licensing, their presence has a knock-on effect. For example, for many university libraries, curating their open access resources is not a priority because fee-paying students have access to those resources anyway. So, there is no real driver for educators to focus on open access above other resources. But when universities started creating MOOC, this placed pressure on people to use open access resources, because the open learners probably wouldn't have library access privileges.

This is similar to the way social media drives open access, because if someone wants to share an article via social media, but then encounters a paywall, most people won't actually access it. What this situation demonstrates is that openness in any form ultimately begets more openness. So, while we may bemoan the fact that MOOC themselves are not really open in the sense of openly licensed, they do form part of a larger system, which helps drive openness. This demonstrates that once the disruption narrative is abandoned, which positions MOOC as competitors to formal higher education, then there are a variety of ways in which they can be complementary.

What MOOC perhaps reveal more clearly are attitudes towards the role of educational technology, as evidenced by the reaction to them. In 2015, I wrote that they appealed to a certain narrative that effectively super-charged the interest in MOOC development:

> I would contend that the reason MOOC attracted so much attention — and so little critical evaluation — is because they slotted neatly into a broader set of narratives, in a way that other forms of open education haven't. There are two aspects to this broader narrative: the first is the framing of the problem as "education is broken," and the second is the overriding Silicon Valley narrative that shapes the form of solutions. (Weller, 2015, p. 119)

In this, they are the prime example of how much of ed tech has been framed in recent years, not as a tool to be used within education but rather as tools to *fix* education. The justification for MOOC was often couched as a response to the rising costs of higher education (e.g., Lawton & Katsomitros, 2012). This argument cites the rising costs of higher education for students, often allied with the declining job market, which situates higher education as a poor return on investment. The proposal made around MOOC, then, was that an efficient, technology-driven solution could therefore reduce much of this excess cost. The same type of efficiency-based argument is sometimes seen with artificial intelligence and learning analytics. This is, obviously, a decidedly neo-liberal interpretation of the function of higher education, but even putting aside that critique, it is also a very U.S.-centric model, where higher education is paid for by students (and also now in the UK). In many countries, higher education is still seen as a public good, and higher education is free, or low cost. Higher education must be paid for somehow, obviously, and is usually financed through government funding, but in such an environment the assumption that students (or consumers) will begin to reject university for the more affordable option simply does not apply. It is telling that in all of the ed tech solutions to the rising cost of higher education, a different model for funding higher education is never proposed; the current student debt-based model is taken as absolute.

Much of this thinking is driven by Christensen's (1997) concept of disruption, which is a much-loved theory in technology companies. Disruption has been widely criticized (Doss, 2014), but it persists as a core idea because it appeals to the narrative myths of the tech industry. However, while it does occur it is actually very rare. And when people talk of disrupting a sector, it is worth questioning if that is really their goal. For example, to disrupt education would mean sweeping away a whole industry. When it does happen, disruption is absolutely merciless — an entire industry is replaced by a new one. The emphasis is not on making improvements (which Christensen (1997) labels as sustaining technology), it is on completely overhauling a sector and replacing it with a new one. For those in that sector, it is effectively an extinction event. For those claiming or desiring disruption, the following three things must hold true:

- A complete, systemic change will overtake the sector.

- The current incumbents will not survive.

- The current incumbents are incapable of accommodating new technology.

This is the core of disruption, so if what is being proposed doesn't entail these radical outcomes, then it's not disruption — it may be technology innovation, it may be new hybrid models, but it is not disruption. If we examine that list with education in mind, then it does not look either desirable or likely. It would mean the closure of schools, colleges, and universities, the redundancy of thousands of educators, and the delivery of all education by new providers. That would be a major social shift and would cause significant upheaval.

One of the methods deployed by promoters of disruption is to label those who disagree with them as resistant to change. Educational technologists can be seen as having a role to play in counteracting this narrative. As a group, they are generally the people who have pushed for change, are keen to embrace technology and to explore possibilities. Their concerns cannot be as easily dismissed as a refusal to accept change or failure to understand the technology. Acting as translators for many of the claims, while also seeing the possibility for new technologies in a practical sense for students will become increasingly important roles for educational technologists.

While the celebrity rise of MOOC has been fascinating to witness, I can't help mourning the move away from the more experimental approach that typified their start. One of the great benefits of early MOOC was that they created a space for educators to explore new pedagogy, technology, or subject matter, without being tied into the conventional restraints of a formal, fee-paying curriculum. The new institutional MOOC became very conventional in their approach and subject matter as the costs of their production rose, and their function as "shop window" came to the fore.

Another misgiving is that, while MOOC are free, they are usually not open in the sense of being reusable and openly accessible. The early MOOC explored the concept of openness in all its interpretations — content, technology, pedagogy, and boundaries. MOOC could have gone down a path where the open aspects were much more prevalent, as with OER. Free access is a significant starting point, but more interesting things happen when MOOC are fully open.

The raised profile of open education and online learning caused by MOOC may be beneficial in the long run, but the MOOC hype may be equally detrimental. The ed tech field needs to learn how to balance these developments. Millions of learners accessing high-quality material online is a positive, but the rush by colleges and universities to enter into prohibitive contracts, outsource expertise, and undermine their own staff has long-term consequences as well. These are all factors that are still playing out.

CHAPTER 20

2013

Open Textbooks

If MOOC were the glamorous side of open education, claiming all the headlines and sweeping predictions, then open textbooks were the practical, even dowdy, application. An extension of the OER movement, and particularly pertinent in the United States and Canada, open textbooks provided openly licensed versions of bespoke written textbooks, with the digital version being free and printed versions at low cost. The price of textbooks has become an increasing issue for North American students, with the average cost per student over US$900 per year (Hilton, Robinson, Wiley, & Ackerman, 2014). This provides an initial opportunity for the OER movement to address a very specific problem and focus on creating openly licensed textbooks. Projects such as OpenStax, the Open Textbook Library, BCcampus, and Lumen Learning are all developing or promoting open textbooks. The findings from these projects have been positive, with research demonstrating the efficacy and quality of such textbooks is as good as, if not better than, existing ones (Fisher, Hilton, Robinson, & Wiley, 2015).

In terms of savings to students, it is difficult to quantify, as usage is not always reported and is thus difficult to track, and although estimates assume all students who downloaded a book would have purchased a new one, they may have opted for cheaper versions, borrowed ones, or decided the textbook was not essential at all. Both OpenStax and BCcampus attempt to accommodate some of this variation by using the average figure of US$100 per textbook per student. With this value OpenStax estimates it has saved students US$155 million in book purchases as of 2018 (OpenStax, 2019) and BCcampus more than CAD$13 million (BCcampus, 2019). Just a single college (De Anza College) estimated savings of US$1 million based on previous purchasing patterns (de los Arcos et al., 2014).

Similarly, Open Up Resources (https://openupresources.org) create open resources that align with the Common Core standard in the United States. These are authored by subject experts, then released as OER. As well as textbooks, Open Up Resources provide supporting material, such as lesson plans, assessments, and family resources. By releasing the content as OER, it can save schools money on purchasing textbooks and also facilitate a more rapid updating and improvement cycle. In South Africa, Siyavula (https://www.siyavula.com) has created open textbooks for maths and science and has worked with the education department to have these distributed. It reports that over 10 million books have been delivered into schools.

These examples illustrate large-scale, if not completely mainstream, adoption of open textbooks to the benefit of thousands of students. Open textbooks have been criticized for being an unimaginative application of the possibilities of the medium and nonetheless coming to dominate the OER field in North America.

Robin DeRosa (2015) has been one of the prominent advocates of open pedagogy, and urges a more radical rethinking of pedagogy, stating that she doesn't "want to be part of a movement that is focused on replacing static, over-priced textbooks with static, free textbooks" (para. 2). Similarly, OER activist Rajiv Jhangiani (2015) suggested that cost should be seen as part of a nuanced message about the benefits of OER that recognizes the heterogeneity of faculty.

Despite these reservations, open textbooks offer a case study of several aspects that need to align for ed tech adoption in higher ed. Firstly, the open education movement set out to establish a solid evidence base. It did not just rely on altruism and statements of belief about the benefits. The Open Education Group at Brigham Young University, in particular, established an evidence base demonstrating that open text-books were of high quality (Bliss, Hilton, Wiley, & Thanos, 2013) and had a positive impact on students (Hilton, 2016). This evidence makes it difficult for them to be dismissed by commercial interests or those who simply want to reject the idea.

Secondly, through the types of projects outlined above, professional, long-term providers were established who could produce textbooks of reliable quality. These books *looked* as good as anything that was purchased, and they didn't appear to have been produced with a DIY approach. This initial reaction to the quality of the physical book is an important aspect for both educators and students. Books are artifacts with which people tend to have an emotional connection.

Thirdly, the switching of costs from purchase to production provides a viable economic model that is applicable for other open approaches. Most of the organizations and projects mentioned above have been supported by philanthropic institutions, such as Shuttleworth, or the Hewlett Foundation. Transitioning to sustainable models poses a challenge. Siyavula, for example, has repositioned itself as a technology company rather than as an open textbook publisher. However, financial models in open education are exploring an "open flip," which sees "a reallocation of finances away from purchasing copyrighted resources to the production of openly licensed ones" (Weller, 2016b, p. 30). For example, the Open Library of Humanities (https://www.openlibhums.org) project operates a range of open access journals in the humanities, with no author facing charges, and is funded by subscriptions from university libraries. Generating such models with the considerable revenue spent in education currently allocated to purchasing copyrighted materials offers potential for considerable savings and the generation of open content.

These three elements of evidence, quality, and economics lay the foundation for the adoption of open textbooks, and they represent a model for how to realize ed tech adoption while avoiding some of the hype and subsequent backlash that has typified other approaches. Now, from this base, the challenge is to start innovating beyond the basic textbook. As with LMS, open textbooks offer an easy route to adoption, and like LMS, the concern is that open textbooks do not act as a stepping-stone to a more innovative, varied teaching approach but rather become an endpoint in themselves. This has led to an exploration of the concept of open pedagogy, which can be defined as teaching approaches that make use of abundant, open content, and which also emphasize the network and the learner's connections within it. Wiley and Hilton (2018) proposed a more OER-centric version of OER-enabled pedagogy, which they defined "as the set of teaching and learning practices that are only possible or practical in the context of the 5R permissions which are characteristic of OER" (p. 135). To meet this definition, they proposed four questions to ask of an approach:

- Are students asked to create new artifacts (essays, poems, videos, songs, etc.) or revise/remix existing OER?

- Does the new artifact have value beyond supporting the learning of its author?

- Are students invited to publicly share their new artifacts or revised/remixed OER?

- Are students invited to openly license their new artifacts or revised/remixed OER? (p. 137)

Similarly, Jhangiani (2017) required students to create test questions to accompany an open textbook they were studying. This deepened the students' understanding and created a pool of questions for subsequent students. DeRosa (2016), likewise, created an open textbook with students and then had each cohort add supplementary material and create introductions to sections to produce a more usable resource. In so doing, the students engaged actively with the text, questioning it and improving it. This changed the way they perceived a textbook: from a vehicle of received knowledge to something they could interact with in a profound way.

But even with these examples, the starting point was usually a desire to save students money. Will the open textbook model transfer when this initial motivation is absent, or not as prominent? The UK Open Textbooks project sought to answer this by adopting the approaches used in the United States for open textbook adoption. In the UK, spending on textbooks is less significant, with students paying out an average of £572 on books and equipment in their first year, falling to £465 in year two and to £490 in year three (Maher et al., 2017). This may not be as high as some U.S. expenditure, but it represents a considerable cost for many students. The use of textbooks in the UK, however, is less directed than in the United States, with students often presented with a reading list rather than a set text (Publishers Association, 2016). Despite these contextual differences, interest in adopting open textbooks has been high, indicating that the model is transferrable. In South Africa, the Digital Open Textbooks for Development (http://www.dot4d.uct.ac.za) project is similarly investigating the potential for open textbooks in their context. This is seen as a means of promoting inclusion and addressing the issue of equitable access. Open textbooks may be set to expand beyond their North American roots, but if the history of the movement is any indication, we should not expect this to be a tale of revolution but rather of slow, steady adoption.

Open textbooks are an example of an ed tech that has been largely driven from inside education itself. It differs in this respect from the sort of ed tech that gets labelled disruptive, as a key component to that narrative is outsiders coming into the education space. As such, open textbooks tend not to attract the sort of venture capital investment or media attention of the more tech-oriented solutions. The movement also doesn't seek to remove the human element from education. The aim is to make education more affordable, flexible, and accessible, but still essentially human.

CHAPTER 21

2014

Learning Analytics

Data, data, data. It's the new oil and the new driver of capitalism, war, and politics, so inevitably its role in education would come to the fore. Interest in analytics is driven by the increased amount of time that students spend in online learning environments, particularly LMS and MOOC, but also the increased data available across a university, including library usage, attendance, demographic data, and so on. Sclater, Peasgood, and Mullan (2016) defined it as "the measurement, collection, analysis and reporting of data about the progress of learners and the contexts in which learning takes place" (p. 4).

Learning analytics grew as a field from around 2011, when George Siemens hosted the first Learning Analytics conference. By 2014, it had emerged as a field of its own, combining elements of statistics, computer science, and education. Although not a direct consequence, there is a definite synergy and similarity between MOOC and learning analytics, not least through the presence of George Siemens as an early and prominent voice in both areas. MOOC generated a lot of interest, partly because they created large datasets, and, partly because, removed from the constraints of formal education, they were vehicles for conducting A/B testing and quantitative analysis. Both approaches brought new people into educational technology, particularly from the computer science field. They brought with them new methods and concepts to apply to educational analysis. If the knowledge exchange is reciprocal, then this evolving nature of ed tech could be one of its strengths.

The positive side of learning analytics is that for distance education, in particular, it provides the equivalent of responding to discreet signals in the face-to-face environment: the puzzled expression, the yawn, or the whispering between students seeking clarity. Every good face-to-face educator will respond to these signals and adjust their behaviour. In an online environment, these cues are absent, and analytics provides some proxy for these. As Siemens and Long (2011) have put it, "Learning analytics can penetrate the fog of uncertainty around how to allocate resources, develop competitive advantages, and most important, improve the quality and value of the learning experience" (p. 40). Bodily, Nyland, and Wiley (2017) proposed the use of analytics to address particular problems, using the RISE (Resource Inspection, Selection, and Enhancement) framework. In this, a 2 × 2 grid of outcome versus engagement was proposed, with a student's grade on assessment on the y-axis, and engagement on the x-axis. By using analytics, educators were able to assess what the authors suggested was the particularly valuable area for intervention — that of high engagement and low attainment.

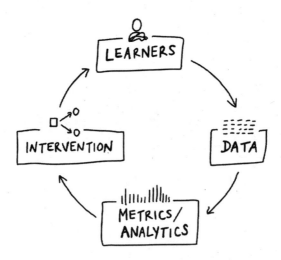

FIGURE 2. The learning analytics cycle, after Clow (2011).

The basic model for analytics allows the identification of issues and then some form of effective intervention is implemented. Clow (2012) proposed a learning analytics cycle, shown in Figure 2. In this model, learners generated data that was then processed into metrics or analytics, such as dashboards. Clow stated that this metrics stage was "the heart of most learning analytics projects and has been the focus of great innovation in tools, methods and methodologies — e.g. dashboards, predictive modelling, social network analysis, recommenders, and so on" (p. 135). For analytics to be effective, however, intervention was required that would have some effect on the behaviour of learners.

Sclater and Mullan (2017) reported on a range of such interventions, usually targeting at-risk students across different institutions, which improved grades in the range of 2 to 12% and increased retention rates. However, analytics can also be used for more long-term analysis. For example, Purdue's Course Signals approach used a traffic light system to predict student performance, based on demographic characteristics, academic history, and interaction with the LMS. Students were sent a personalized email from the faculty member that indicated their "traffic signal colour." Their results showed improved retention and generally high levels of student satisfaction (Arnold & Pistilli, 2012). However, the validity of some of these results was called into question. Caulfield (2013b) highlighted that with more Course Signals courses in existence, students who persisted would inevitably take more such courses: "Students are taking more...Signals courses because they persist, rather than persisting because they are taking more Signals courses" (para. 7). This highlights two issues with analytics: firstly, that their claims are often difficult for non-experts to verify, and secondly that a problem existed around correlation and causation. It is no surprise that students who perform better tend to spend more time in the library or contribute more in the LMS. These are attributes of studying, so "good" students tend to study a lot. But making other students spend more time in the LMS, for example, may not lead to an improvement in performance.

Rienties (2018) used analysis of different large data sets at the Open University to highlight "6 myths" or commonly held beliefs about student behaviour:

- Open University (OU) students love to work together.

- Student satisfaction is positively related to success.

- Student performance improves over time (e.g., from first to third level courses).

- The grades students achieve are mostly related to what they do.

- Student engagement in the VLE is mostly determined by the student.

- Most OU students follow the schedule when studying.

The data reveals that all these preconceptions are, to some extent, false. What this analysis reveals could be deemed as concerns, but it also highlights positive behaviour. For example, that student behaviour is largely determined by what is set out in the course (number 5) can be interpreted as an effective outcome of good learning design, particularly for distance education students. Similarly, while students don't slavishly follow the course schedule (number 6), with many studying ahead or just behind the calendar, this can be framed as part of the flexible (and accessible) design. What this type of analysis highlights is the value in questioning our assumptions about student behaviour. Just as an author may have their ideal reader in mind, a course designer may have an ideal student, but this analysis reveals that some of those assumptions may not be valid.

The downsides to learning analytics are that they can reduce students to data and that ownership of this data becomes a commodity in itself. The use of data surveillance has only just begun and with scandals around Facebook and Cambridge Analytica (see for example, Cadwalldr & Graham-Harrison, 2018), the issues involved in how data is used are only just becoming apparent. Higher education has a duty to increase understanding about these data-harvesting activities, and it should not be seen to be partaking in data surveillance and accustoming students to this way of working unquestioningly. Analytics puts the institution in the position of the central panopticon, potentially observing all student interaction (Land & Bayne, 2005). The ed tech field needs to avoid the mistakes of data capitalism and should embed learner agency and ethics in the use of data, and it should deploy that data sparingly. Nelson and Harfield (2017) claimed that it is essential for students to be involved in the discussions about analytics, stating that the primary aim of a university education is "to ethically develop and realize both individual and socio-cultural potentialities ... that can only happen when students are involved in making sense of their own data" (para. 02).

Another implication is that a data-driven approach is essentially a quantitative field, but education is largely a qualitative one, dealing with real students, in something that is of great emotional significance. It can sometimes be easy to forget that the nodes on a data plot are students. We are only at the beginning of the use of analytics in education, and as the quantity of data and the sophistication of the analysis increases, the danger is that instead of analytics supporting education, analytics *becomes* education.

In order to realize a moral implementation of learning analytics and address some of these issues, Slade and Prinsloo (2013) propose six principles:

- Learning analytics as moral practice — their first principle is to appreciate that learning analytics is a moral undertaking and should not only focus on what is effective, but also "function primarily as a moral practice resulting in understanding rather than measuring" (p. 12).

- Students as agents — in line with Nelson and Harfield (2017), they propose that institutions should "engage students as collaborators and not as mere recipients of interventions and services" (p. 12).

- Student identity and performance are temporal dynamic constructs — students' identities will change over the course of their studies; indeed, education is often portrayed as an identity changing experience. Analytics and data need to take this into account.

- Student success is a complex and multidimensional phenomenon — student success and behaviour is a result of more than can be measured through data.

- Transparency — institutions should be transparent regarding what data is gathered and how it will be used.

- Higher education cannot afford to not use data — however, they stress that it is part of an institution's responsibility to make moral and effective use of data.

As Slade and Prinsloo (2013) have pointed out, there are serious ethical issues raised by analytics, which current legislation and systems may be ill-equipped to deal with. Let's imagine a scenario where a researcher has created a very accurate predictive analytics model that can foretell whether a student will drop out or complete a course with something approaching 90% accuracy. For this scenario, let us put aside debate about whether this is possible, although Agnihotri and Ott (2014) reported a 75% accurate predictive model for students who do not return. The researcher's intentions are entirely noble — the researcher wants to allow the university to target extra support for these students to increase their chances of success. This, however, immediately raises an ethical problem: Should the students be told? Would this make it a self-fulfilling prophecy? Clow (2013) summarized it thus:

> What is the ethical thing to do when your predictive algorithm says there's very little chance that a would-be student will pass your course? Is it right to take their time, effort and money (or that of whoever is subsidising their place), when it will almost certainly come to very little? But on the other hand, is it right to block them from study? (para. 4)

Moving beyond this immediate concern, let's assume this algorithm gets adopted in a learning analytics system taken up by universities worldwide. Any such algorithm will likely incorporate elements of class and race, or at least proxies for these; for example, Sclater (2014) reported on a university's use of analytics to specifically offer tailored support for black and minority ethnic students. For many universities in our scenario, rather than being a means of offering extra support, it allows them to more accurately filter out students who are expensive to support and more likely to fail. When universities are judged on their completion and continuation rates (for example, continuation is one of the metrics in the teaching excellence framework in the UK), then such action becomes more likely.

Our intrepid researcher, who started out wanting to increase the support for disadvantaged students, is now the cause of a global system that is reinforcing privilege and creating an elitist education system, which systematically excludes certain groups. Algorithms are not apolitical. While there are, of course, many assumptions and over-simplifications in this scenario that could be challenged, its function is to highlight how even well-intentioned applications of analytics can quickly raise very complex ethical questions.

One of the benefits of considering analytics might simply be better communication with students. Navigating the peculiar, often idiosyn-cratic, world of higher education with its rules and regulations can be daunting and confusing. By considering useful dashboards, for instance, the complexity of this is surfaced. Bennett (2018), for example, reported how the items most valued by students were clear graphics showing attendance and predicted degree grade. The latter was not based on behavioural analytics but rather a calculation based on their scores in modules so far. With different weightings, substitutions, and averaging, it is often difficult for a student to know what degree of classification they are on track for, and what improvements they need to make in terms of scores in order to adjust this. This highlights how institutions can do a lot to simplify and communicate their processes to students.

Analytics and data are in the early stages of their adoption, and as Slade and Prinsloo (2013) proposed, institutions cannot afford *not* to use them. It is difficult to argue that you make education more effective by knowing less about your students, but the usage of analytics comes with a host of issues that are complex to navigate. Probably more than any other ed tech application, learning analytics necessitates a moral philosopher or social scientist in the room alongside the developers.

CHAPTER 22

2015

Digital Badges

Providing digital badges for achievements that can be verified and linked to evidence started with Mozilla's open badge infrastructure (https://openbadges.org/) in 2011, with IMS taking over the badges standard in 2017 (IMS, 2017). An open standard is crucial for badges because it means that anyone can create them, thus they can be used by formal accrediting agencies, such as schools and universities, but also informal ones, such as online communities or employers. Gibson, Ostashewski, Flintoff, Grant, and Knight (2015) defined them as "a representation of an accomplishment, interest or affiliation that is visual, available online, and contains metadata including links that help explain the context, meaning, process and result of an activity" (p. 404).

Digital badges are a good example of how ed tech evolves when several other technologies, such as those that we have seen in this book, make the environment favourable for their implementation. The process of plant succession provides a useful analogy (Weller, 2007b).

> When there is a new environment, for example barren rock, a few pioneer species like lichens begin to grow. The acid from lichens decomposes some rock particles, and their own death creates a coarse soil. This soil is suitable for mosses that require little soil, and they, in turn, decompose to enrich and deepen the

> soil until it is suitable for some grasses to grow. The process ends with the establishment of a stable, climax community. (p. 43)

In the same manner, the presence of some technologies changes the environment sufficiently that it makes it favourable for other technologies. The success of that technology is not inevitable, but it does make the context more suitable. For digital badges, several technologies coalesced to provide this favourable environment. From social media and Web 2.0, a familiarity with sharing and developing online identity was acquired. Blogs and e-portfolios provided a platform for showcasing digital outputs. Gaming provided the concept of rewards, tokens, and status while online review systems, such as Amazon, raised the reputational profile. OER and MOOC created a large informal learning population who wished to have their achievements recognized. Open source and other online communities demonstrated how kudos could be given to users who had assumed specific roles within the group. All of these elements then combined to create an environment in which digital badges could be seen as a response to a range of needs, and the concept had sufficient links into everyday practice, such as sharing on social networks, to have a chance of success.

Badges allow for a more fine-grained representation of skills and experience gained in formal education than a degree classification. In this, they are an extension of the desire of e-portfolios to surface skills and competencies that are useful to employers. Examples of badges, taken from the IMS specification (IMS, 2017), include e-publishing, success in challenge-based learning, knowledge of data science foundations, pipetting skills, and so on.

Badges can also provide motivation, in line with gamification: the theory is that small rewards at regular intervals incentivize desirable behaviour. The use of badges can reportedly lead to increased participation and changes in behaviour on a site (Anderson, Huttenlocher, Kleinberg, & Leskovec, 2013), although Ambrose, Anthony, and Clark (2016) reported no difference in completion rates between students who were offered badges on a MOOC and those who were not. In contrast, Law (2015) reported that badged open courses have shown a higher completion rate. It is, however, not a straightforward matter that badges increase motivation. In seeking to answer the question, "Are badges useful in education?" Abramovich, Schunn, and Higashi (2013) found different responses for low- and high-performing students, and for different types of badges. For example, they found that "only for the low-performing students in [their] study did a higher desire to outperform other students, the performance approach goal, correlate with earning more badges" (p. 229).

Like many other ed tech developments, digital badges had an initial flurry of interest from devotees but then settled into a pattern of more labourious long-term acceptance. They represent a combination of key challenges for educational technology: realizing easy-to-use, scalable technology; developing social awareness that gives them currency; and providing the policy and support structures that make them valuable.

Of these challenges, only the first relates directly to technology, the more substantial ones relate to awareness and legitimacy. For example, if employers or institutions come to widely accept and value digital badges, then they will gain credence with learners who will seek them out, creating a virtuous circle. There is some movement in this area. IBM, for example, uses badges in its staff development system (Jackson, 2017). Raish and Rimland (2016) reported that only 5% of surveyed employers said they weren't interested in digital badges, and there was particular interest in them as a means to make certain skills explicit that they felt graduates lacked,

> the three areas where employers least expect students to have competency are the ability to find patterns and make connections (18%), the ability to apply knowledge to real-world contexts (29%), and the ability to work with people from diverse backgrounds (29%). (p. 99)

But as with e-portfolios, employers may say they want digital badges, but this does not mean they will necessarily change practice to utilize them. Badges do not usually have the same level of assessment effort attached to them as graded work, and so there is a possibility that they may not differentiate sufficiently; for example, everyone who graduates acquires the information literacy badge. This would then require potential employers to have to examine the supporting evidence and make assessments on its quality, and this represents an additional burden in the recruitment process that they are unlikely to adopt.

The credibility issue is also one of the main concerns for those gaining badges, as Davis and Singh (2015) reported, "while participants recognized the value in being able to document students' afterschool learning and share it with a wide audience, they noted the difficulty of having this new form of credential recognized widely as legitimate, trustworthy evidence of students' skills and achievements" (p. 80). The technical infrastructure goes some way to assuring this credibility. This is achieved by means of our friend from chapter 8, metadata. The digital badge contains metadata about the learner, the issuer of the badge, a link to the evidence, criteria for acquiring the badge, etc. This means anyone viewing the badge can verify its authenticity.

Perhaps more interesting is what happens when educators design for badges, breaking courses down into smaller chunks with associated recognition. For example, Brandman University (2015) partnered with badge provider Credly to offer badges to complement a competency-based approach. Coughlan, Pitt, and McAndrew (2013) reported how they converted an existing foundation-level maths course into OER, and they associated tasks along the way with badges. As with many ed tech approaches, such as the use of OER, it may be that one of the benefits of badges is that they cause educators to reflect on their own practice. Badge-based approaches can help to structure courses into manageable chunks, with convenient rewards along the way.

Another growing use of badges is as a means of recognizing much of the hidden work in academia. For example, the Association for Learning Technology Conference offers badges to speakers, reviewers, session chairs, members of the organizing committee, and blog contributors.

The adoption of digital badges is a familiar theme in ed tech, and they have realized considerable success, if not quite the mainstream adoption once envisaged. The reaction to them from learners is predictably mixed — some are keen to collect as many badges as possible, while others view them as trivial and irrelevant. Like so many approaches in ed tech, it may be that they don't need to be for everyone, but for a certain group of learners, they provide motivation, reward, and structure to learning that they value.

CHAPTER 23

2016

The Return of Artificial Intelligence

Artificial intelligence (AI) is an interesting case study in ed tech, combining several themes that have already arisen in this book: promise versus reality, the cyclical nature of ed tech, and the increasingly thorny ethical issues raised by its application. The possibilities of AI in education saw an early burst of enthusiasm in the 1980s, particularly with the concept of Intelligent Tutoring Systems (ITS). This initial enthusiasm waned somewhat in the 1990s. This was mainly because ITS only worked for very limited, tightly specified domains. Developers needed to predict the types of errors people would make in order to provide advice on how to rectify these. And in many subjects (the humanities in particular), it transpired that people could be very creative in the errors they made, and more significantly, what constituted the right answer was less well defined. For example, in their influential paper, Anderson, Boyle, and Reiser (1985) detailed intelligent tutoring systems for geometry and the programming language LISP (derived from "list processor"). They confidently predicted that "cognitive psychology, artificial intelligence, and computer technology have advanced to the point where it is feasible to build computer systems that are as effective as intelligent human tutors" (p. 456).

Yet, by 1997, Anderson and his colleagues (Corbett, Koedinger, & Anderson, 1997) were among those lamenting that "intelligent tutoring has had relatively little impact on education and training in the world" (p. 850). In their analysis they hit upon something which seems obvious, and yet continues to echo through educational technology, namely that the technology (in this case intelligent tutoring systems, but it might equally apply to MOOC, say) has not been developed according to educational perspectives. They stated:

> The creative vision of intelligent computer tutors has largely arisen among artificial intelligence researchers rather than education specialists. Researchers recognized that intelligent tutoring systems are a rich and important natural environment in which to deploy and improve AI algorithms… the bottom line is that intelligent tutoring systems are generally evaluated according to artificial intelligence criteria… rather than with respect to a cost/benefit analysis educational effectiveness. (p. 851)

In short, the technology is developed and evaluated by people who like the technology but don't have an appreciation of the educational context. In this snapshot, we have much of the history of ed tech.

In the 1990s, while issues with ITS were becoming apparent, there was a second flush of popularity around AI in general, focused on the potential of two approaches: expert systems and neural networks. These were contrasting approaches: expert systems sought to explicitly capture expertise in the form of rules, whereas neural networks learned from inputs in a manner analogous to the brain. They can be viewed as top-down and bottom-up approaches respectively.

Expert systems were primarily focused on problem solving and diagnosis, but they had potential as teaching aids also—if the knowledge of an expert in, say, medical diagnosis, could be captured effectively, then this would form a useful teaching aid, particularly for problem-based approaches to education. While expert systems could perform reasonably well within constrained domains, they did not achieve a major impact in education. The problem was twofold:

the oft-quoted "knowledge acquisition bottleneck" (e.g., Wagner, 2006; Cullen & Bryman, 1998) and the complexity of real-world domains. The knowledge acquisition bottleneck refers to the difficulty in acquiring knowledge from experts (or other resources) in a format that can be represented in an expert system. It is not possible to simply extract the knowledge from an expert like siphoning petrol from a car, and so it requires lengthy interviews or observations.

Experts don't always agree and making expertise explicit is notoriously difficult. What often characterizes an expert is that they "just know." For instance, chess experts will be able to reproduce a board they are shown much better than you could (assuming you're not a chess expert, that is). The reason is that they encode it as patterns linked to long-term memory, whereas novices are encoding it as discrete elements, for example, the white rook is next to the black pawn two spaces in. Experts don't know how they do this, it arises as a by-product of expertise — they don't explicitly intend to encode in this manner, but it is what they do as they gain expertise (Chi, Glaser, & Farr, 2014). Interestingly, if you show expert chess players a random placement of figures, that is, they are not real mid-game positions, then they recall them with the same accuracy as everyone else. What this means for AI is that acquiring the knowledge from experts into an encodable form is time consuming and not always an accurate representation of what they know.

The complexity issue means that the world will operate in unpredictable ways. For example, I developed an expert system for diagnosing flaws in an aluminium die-casting system (Webster, Weller, Sfantsikopoulos, & Tsoukalas, 1993). This worked tolerably well, by characterizing typical flaws, but sometimes these flaws co-occurred, sometimes they appeared differently, and often the causes of the flaws were multiple. To borrow a term from software engineering, expert systems, and intelligent tutoring systems, the system did not "degrade gracefully." In software, this refers to the ability of a system to maintain limited functionality even when a large portion of it is inoperative or under heavy load. In early expert systems, it might be interpreted as the system either knew or it didn't know. Humans are very good at degrading gracefully (and sometimes disgracefully too), so they can take a good guess based on experience.

What is of general interest is that the current claims of AI are much the same and that some of the problems remain. However, what has really changed in the interim is the power of computation. This helps address some of the complexity issues because multiple possibilities and probabilities can be accommodated. In this we see a recurring theme in ed tech: nothing changes while simultaneously everything changes. AI has definitely improved since the 1980s, but some of the fundamental issues that beleaguered it remain.

In an analysis of AI in education, Roll and Wylie (2016) identified several trends since its early implementation, including an increase in the empirical evaluation of tools. This is another universal trend in ed tech — early research tends to focus on potential and possibility, but gradually more critical perspectives are brought to bear, and the need for reliable evidence becomes prominent. This same pattern has been seen in OER (Weller, 2016a) and learning analytics (Gasevic, Siemens, & Rosé, 2017). Roll and Wylie (2016) also reported an increased discussion on the theoretical implications, a focus on STEM applications, and the development of step-based systems rather than complex domains. This represents a narrowing of focus for ITS away from the broader claims of being applicable to all subjects and of replacing teachers, to a more practical implementation centred on approaches and subjects where there is evidence of success. Roll and Wylie summarized the evolution of AI in education stating that it has been "focusing on a very specific scenario, and has been doing it well: the use of computers in the classroom to teach domain knowledge in STEM topics using step-based problems" (p. 590). Again, this is symptomatic of much of ed tech — initial hype and claims of revolution followed by a sequence of more tightly focused adoption within the existing educational framework.

AI has definitely improved since the 1990s, though, and perhaps most significantly it has become prevalent in much of our daily lives: credit assessment, technical troubleshooting, voice recognition systems such as Siri, and computer games all rely on aspects of AI. It is important to distinguish, however, between narrow and general AI. These applications are all examples, however effective, of narrow AI, which means they can perform one aspect of human functioning pretty well but cannot generalize. They are designed for a specific purpose and have no ambition to go beyond those narrow boundaries. This type of AI will likely proliferate, and its application in education has potential, as the review above indicates. By concentrating on narrow tasks, good performance can be realized. For example, language learning bots, sophisticated automatic assessment, resource recommenders, and so forth can all be deployed within an existing educational ecosystem.

This narrow AI is very distinct from the type of AI that most people call to mind, and which tends to attract headlines, which is a more general AI. The aim of general AI is to develop systems that can generalize and perform any intellectual task that a human being can. Successful applications of general AI are rare to non-existent — which is not to say there won't be a world of Blade Runner-type replicants one day, but it is unlikely to arrive any time soon, and if it does arrive, the social impacts will be far beyond education. Selwyn (2018) proposed six reasons why artificial intelligence technology will never take over from human teachers:

- Human teachers have learned what they know.

- Human teachers make cognitive connections.

- Human teachers make social connections.

- Human teachers talk out loud.

- Human teachers perform with their bodies.

- Human teachers improvise and "make do."

This list can be seen as more of an argument against general AI than against particular narrow AI tools. It also repeats some of the elitism against distance education that was evident in early e-learning criticisms — the idea that face-to-face, real-time education is the only true form of learning is evident in claims such as "teachers perform with their bodies." However, the flexibility, emotional, and cognitive connections that learners make with human educators is an important aspect of the educational process. It is why education has been so resistant to a formula for success — it is a fundamentally human experience.

More significant than the technological issues are the ethical ones. As Audrey Watters (2017) has contended, "Artificial intelligence is not developed in a vacuum. AI isn't simply technological: it's ideological" (para 1). We shall return to the social implications of algorithms and black box approaches when we discuss 2018 in chapter 25, but the more authority and power we allocate to AI systems, which we cannot "see inside of," the more possibilities for real-life negative effects arise from these systems that cannot be explained, tracked, or held accountable. The concern about AI is not that it won't deliver on the promise held forth by its advocates but rather that someday it will. And then the assumptions embedded in code will shape how education is realized, and if learners don't fit that conceptual model, they will find themselves outside of the area in which compassion will allow a human to intervene. Perhaps the greatest contribution of AI will be to make us realize how important people truly are in the education system.

CHAPTER 24

2017

Blockchain

Of all the technologies covered in this book, blockchain is perhaps the most perplexing, both in how it works and in terms of its purpose in education. I include it because it received a lot of attention, but also because it is indicative of the type of hype that surrounds a new technology that does not seem to address a clear need. Let's address the technical part first, although part of blockchain's appeal is in *not* understanding how it works, which we shall come to later. Tapscott and Tapscott (2016) defined blockchain as "an incorruptible digital ledger of economic transactions that can be programmed to record not just financial transactions but virtually everything of value" (p. 5). They argued that "as a decentralised system, it can't be hacked, and it enables you to bypass the complex network of intermediaries currently needed to verify transactions" (p. 5). A blockchain is formed from a database that is shared across a network of computers. These networks are public but encrypted, so when an update is made to the database, such as a new transaction, it is automatically updated across the network. This distributed nature makes it very difficult to hack since any hacker would need to make changes across the network. Cryptocurrencies such as Bitcoin use blockchain to create a ledger that holds the records of Bitcoin transactions. The lack of a central location storing this database makes it secure and ideal for online, peer-to-peer transactions.

If you are thinking that this all sounds fine for finance, but what has it got to do with education, students, and learning, then you are not alone. In 2016 several people independently approached me about blockchain, and their question was always the same: "Could we apply this in education somehow?" The imperative seemed to be that blockchain was an interesting technology, and therefore it must have an educational application. In a review of its possible applications in education, Grech and Camilleri (2017) proposed four possible areas of impact:

- A system for certification — Records of achievement could be securely stored via blockchain. This could be expanded to include credit transfer and recognition of informal learning.

- Verification of validity — Users can automatically check the validity of certificates, without the need to contact the issuing organization that originally issued them.

- Ownership of data — Users could potentially gain increased ownership and control over their own data, which would reduce the data management costs for universities.

- Cryptocurrency payments — Institutions and individuals can use cryptocurrency payment methods, which could enhance grant or voucher-based funding models.

Similarly, Fagan (2018) reported on several university pilots and start-ups experimenting with blockchain approaches for credentialing and recognizing competency-based achievements, and the University of Bahrain announced that it was using blockchain to provide all students with a digital record of achievement (Galea-Pace, 2019).

Viewed in this way, blockchain could be seen as a means of bringing together several of the preceding technologies: e-portfolios, with the aim to provide an individual, portable record of educational achievement; digital badges, with the intention to recognize informal learning; MOOC and OER, with the desire to offer varied informal learning opportunities; and PLE and personalized learning, with the idea of focusing more on the individual than on an institution. A personal, secure, permanent, and portable ledger may well be the ring to bind all these together. However, examining the list of applications above, many of them could be realized with existing technology, such as a conventional database with personal encryption. As Orlowski (2018) bemoaned: "Any claim made for blockchain could be made for databases, or simply publishing contractual or transactional data gathered in another form" (para. 8).

In addition, the trumpeted security of blockchain comes at a huge environmental cost. As the ledger grows, so it is distributed across more and more computers, and these all need to be updated any time a transaction is completed. The energy consumption required for this is staggering, as Reed (2017) has claimed:

> If Bitcoin's network were a country, it would rank 60th in terms of global energy consumption, on par with the nation of Bulgaria. The energy used by a single Bitcoin transaction could power the average U.S. household for eight days. (para. 2)

More environmentally-friendly methods are proposed, such as deploying unused storage on hard drives (Jackson, 2018), but given the inherent energy demands in blockchain, it would seem a strange choice on which to base a global education ledger when we are seeking to reduce such consumption.

The history of the related technologies listed above should also be a warning for blockchain enthusiasts. With e-portfolios, for instance, even when there is a very clear and reasonable connection to educational practice, adoption can be slow, requiring many other components to fall into place. In 2018, even the relatively conservative and familiar educational technology of open textbooks is far from being broadly accepted. Therefore, attempting to convince educators that a complex technology might solve a problem they don't think they have is unlikely to meet with widespread support.

If blockchain is to realize any success, it will need to work almost unnoticed; it will succeed only if people don't know they're using blockchain. Nevertheless, many who propose blockchain display a definite evangelist's zeal; they desire its adoption as an end goal in itself, rather than as an appropriate solution to a specific problem. Many of the impacts suggested above have the air of looking for a problem that blockchain could solve, rather than existing problems for which the technology is the ideal solution. Offering students access to a digital record of achievement, for example, will become increasingly common-place, and blockchain provides a means of realizing this. However, a trusted, encrypted database from a university would achieve much of the same. As with MOOC, what is evident in much of the blockchain hype is that rebranding fairly conventional offerings with the new term generates media coverage and provides an image of innovation. For example, existing online courses were rebranded as SPOC (small, private online courses) in an attempt to acquire some of the techno-logical glow of MOOC.

Similarly, we will see fairly conventional database methods rebranded as blockchain initiatives. I received an email recently encour-aging me to purchase the world's first blockchain craft beer, which would allow me to track the source of all the ingredients. This could be easily realized previously (but no one thought it was particularly worthwhile), yet the lure of adding blockchain to the process somewhere was too great for this company. I can't verify whether it enhanced the flavour of the beer, however, as I resisted the urge to buy.

Beyond this labelling, there is a tendency to promote blockchain as a magical solution for all manner of problems. For instance, the former UK Chancellor of the Exchequer, Phillip Hammond, suggested it was the means to solve the potential border issue with Ireland in the event of the UK leaving the European Union, stating, "I don't claim to be an expert on it but the most obvious technology is blockchain" (Cellan-Jones, 2018, para. 3). How blockchain would realize this and overcome the far larger social issues that would need to be resolved in order for the blockchain to be effective was not made clear. It was a mythical solution.

Maintaining this aura of magic is not accidental. Blockchain is after all a solution that will be sold by providers, and transparency and understanding are not always in their interest. In an analysis of 43 blockchain applications, Burg, Murphy, and Pétraud (2018) found "no documentation or evidence of the results blockchain was purported to have achieved" (para. 5). None of the providers offering solutions were willing to share data, results, or processes. The authors concluded that "despite all the hype about how blockchain will bring unheralded transparency to processes and operations in low-trust environments, the industry is itself opaque" (para. 6).

Blockchain can be seen as the latest instantiation of a recurring theme in ed tech, which can be termed "technology as alchemy." The history of much of chemistry was plagued by the completely false notion of alchemy and the idea that base metals could be transmuted into gold. This dominated any experimentation in chemistry for centuries and reappeared in different cultures and at different times. The dogged pursuit of alchemy was characterized by the following:

Greed — Unlimited wealth awaited the successful alchemist.

Obfuscation — Alchemy persisted through rumour and secret formulas, adding to its allure. The process was never made public.

Magical lexicon — This obfuscation worked not only by being secretive but by creating a language that was difficult to penetrate.

Vagueness — Although the ultimate aim of producing gold was clear, it was accompanied by vagueness regarding other benefits, including immortality, spiritual awakening, and improved health.

Occasional side benefits — Almost inevitably given the time devoted to it, there was the occasional chemical breakthrough which occurred as a side benefit of alchemy, such as, the discovery of phosphorus.

Persistence despite results — Despite the obvious lack of success people persisted, and indeed this complete lack of success was only seen as a reason to continue. Succeeding where others had failed represented an irresistible challenge and some of the best minds in history (such as Isaac Newton) were involved in this fruitless pursuit.

While blockchain is not as nonsensical as alchemy, there are similarities with how it is sold and portrayed. Blockchain is by no means alone in employing an alchemic mindset in its promotion — proponents of AI, learning analytics, and automatic assessment could all be said to deploy similar tactics. From the perspective of blockchain, we can consider the similarities with my alchemy list:

Greed — The education market is estimated at $6 trillion annually and selling a universal solution across all providers that is linked to their most treasured asset (accreditation) would provide significant returns.

Obfuscation — It is frequently made obscure by commercial interests with black box algorithms. As the study above highlights, they report questionable results which are difficult to verify and do not share their data.

Magical lexicon — It has its own lexicon of algorithms, ledgers, and encryption that increasingly begins to look like magic to outsiders.

Vagueness — There is often a vagueness around improved efficiency, learner agency, lifelong learning, and so on. The four potential impacts suggested by Grech and Camilleri (2017) indicate some of these ill-defined possible benefits, such as improved efficiency in institutions' data management systems.

Side benefits — Perhaps not accidentally, but amidst all the investment, it is likely there will be some practical advantages of blockchain, which will be over-reported. For instance, instant access to trusted digital certificates without the need to contact institutions will benefit refugees whose original paper certificates may have been lost or destroyed.

Persistence — Watters (2013b) has talked of "zombie ideas" in ed tech that just refuse to die. Automatic tuition and micro-credentialing are amongst these, and blockchain represents the latest technology to offer a solution for these ideas.

This is not to suggest that blockchain cannot be successfully implemented and possibly solve very specific issues that provide real benefits for learners. The objection here is to the overblown claims and the often-unspoken alchemical tradition that persists in ed tech, of which blockchain is merely the latest realization. The effective way to combat this is through openness (of data, algorithms, claims, and results), focusing on very specific problems to address (instead of grand revolutions) and bringing a critical perspective to any "magical" solutions.

As with alchemy, the danger is that there will be wasted time, effort, and money in the pursuit of an unattainable goal instead of focusing on smaller, achievable ones. Just as with alchemy, once experimenters stopped trying to produce gold, they went on to discover elements, invent medicines, and create all manner of new materials that could be used every day. As educational technologists, then, we should always be wary of any technology that has the whiff of alchemy about it, and the traits above provide a useful checklist against which to review any technological solution.

CHAPTER 25

2018

Ed Tech's Dystopian Turn

For this final year of the 25, a trend rather than a technology is the focus. There is in much of ed tech a growing divide, particularly in evidence at conferences. One camp is largely uncritical, seeing ed tech as a sort of Silicon Valley-inspired, technological utopia that will cure all of education's problems. This is often a reflection-free zone, because the whole basis of this industry is built on selling perfect solutions, often to problems that have been artificially concocted. In contrast to this is a developing strand of criticality around the role of technology in society and in education in particular. This camp can sometimes be guilty of being overly critical, seeking reasons to refute every technology and dismiss any change. However, with the impact of social media on politics, Russian bots, disinformation, data surveillance, and numerous privacy scares, the need for a critical approach is apparent. Being skeptical about technology can no longer be seen as a specialist interest.

This criticality comes in many forms. One prominent strand of such an approach is suspicion about the claims of educational technology in general, and the role of software companies in particular, as we saw with the assertions relating to blockchain. One of the consequences of ed tech entering the mainstream of education is that it becomes increasingly attractive to companies that wish to join the lucrative education market. Much of the narrative around ed tech is associated with change, which quickly becomes co-opted into broader agendas around commercialization, commodification, and massification of education.

For instance, in their report, "An Avalanche Is Coming," Barber, Donnelly, and Rizvi (2013) argued that systemic change in higher education is inevitable because education — perceived as slow, resistant to change, and old-fashioned — is seen as ripe for disruption, and ed tech is the means through which such change is realized. Increasingly, then, academic ed tech is reacting against these claims about the role of technology and is questioning the impacts on learner and scholarly practice, as well as the long-term implications for education in general. For example, in learning analytics we saw that academics are questioning the ethical framework and seeking to influence the field for the benefit of learners.

One of the key voices in ed tech criticality is Neil Selwyn (2014), who argued that engaging with the digital impact on education in a critical manner is a key role of educators, stating "the notion of a contemporary educational landscape infused with digital data raises the need for detailed inquiry and critique" (p. 68) This includes being self-critical and analyzing the assumptions and progress in movements within ed tech. It is important to distinguish critique as Selwyn sees it from the posture of simply being anti-technology or putting forward a blanket resistance to any change. It is a mistake to position these views in pro- and anti-technology camps, and indeed such a positioning is often deployed by vendors of ed tech to pressure uptake of their solution, with the implicit, and sometimes explicit, argument that someone is either stuck in the past and resistant to technology or they are forward-looking and progressive, and therefore keen to adopt their technology. Associating technology adoption with positive characteristics and criticism with negative ones is not a new marketing technique. The stance of criticality vis-à-vis ed tech should be seen as a more nuanced view than this — one can still be enthusiastic about the application of technology to benefit learners while being aware of the broader implications, questioning claims, and advocating (or conducting) research about real impacts.

While there are many flavours of criticality in educational technol-ogy, and we have seen a number of these related to specific technologies in the preceding chapters, by focusing on the work of three critical voices in ed tech some broader principles can be extracted that are not linked to just one technology.

The first of these voices relates to the invasive uses of technologies, many of which are co-opted into education, which highlights the import-ance of developing an understanding of how data is used. Chris Gilliard (2017) monitored the invasive applications of technology and curated a list of reports detailing such uses of technology, which included:

Facebook outs sex workers (Hill, 2017) — By using algorithms unknown to the user, sex workers with two identities found that Facebook connected these and suggested their "real" identity to clients.

Uber's creepy stalker view — At a party, the Uber CEO allegedly treated guests to a display of the "creepy stalker view, showing them the whereabouts and movements of 30 Uber users in New York in real time" (Hill, 2014).

Amazon's remote deletion of *1984* (Manjoo, 2009) — In one of the most ironic accounts of privacy invasion, Amazon deleted purchased copies of Orwell's *1984* from Kindle, removing copies without the permission or knowledge of users.

The use of big data to predict employee sickness (Silverman, 2016) — "Employee wellness firms" and insurers mined data about individual's prescription drugs, and shopping habits to predict which workers would have health problems.

Facial recognition in church (Bailey, 2015) — A company offered churches facial recognition software so they could track who attended services.

Disneyland's electronic whip (Allen, 2011) — Workers at
Disneyland in Florida had their data displayed on public,
flat-screen monitors. The display listed workers by name,
so their colleagues could compare work speeds.

The company that searches social media for brand risk —
The software company Fama (https://www.fama.io) claimed
to apply machine learning to social media content to identify
any history of anti-social behaviour in potential employees.

While any one of these accounts may be exaggerated, justified, or since
rectified, in combination they reveal a society where data can be used
in unexpected ways, for purposes that the individual cannot control.
While these examples are not in ed tech, it is not difficult to imagine
versions of them in education.

Beyond privacy issues, Watters (2018b) compiled a list of the nefarious social and political uses or connections of educational technology,
either technology designed for education specifically or co-opted into
educational purposes. These included:

Border surveillance — The entrepreneur who developed the
popular virtual reality software Oculus, was reportedly
developing software to monitor and identify illegal border
crossings from Mexico to the U.S. (Levy, 2018).

AI to deprofessionalize teachers — AI researcher and former
Google executive Kai-Fu Lee set out how he envisaged AI
applications in China would allow for 1,000-to-1 student-to-
teacher ratios, monitor attendance using facial recognition,
and ensure certain students learn from a select group of
masters (Corcoran, 2018).

Links between the far right and blockchain — Golumbia (2018)
detailed the philosophical underpinnings of much of the
cryptocurrency movements, including their dependency on

"right-wing and often anti-Semitic conspiracy theories about
the nature of central banking" (para. 23).

YouTube's role in radicalization — The recommendation engine
of YouTube accelerates the move to extreme content, so that
a user might find they are quickly presented with conspiracy
theories and radicalizing content. Tufecki (2018) reported
this happens for both left- and right-wing politics, stating
that "YouTube was recommending content that was more and
more extreme than the mainstream political fare I had started
with" (para. 4). This algorithmic recommendation of polarizing
content is addressed in more detail below.

Algorithms that reinforce social bias — An experimental
machine-learning algorithm was tested by Amazon to help
select the best applicants for jobs, but it began to exhibit
bias against female applicants, because it learned from,
and reinforced, previous bias in selection procedures
(Vincent, 2018).

As with the previous list, it is not any individual story in the above
list that is significant, but rather the general pattern the stories reveal.
For example, it might not be too significant for ed tech that YouTube
has been put to nefarious uses by some — *Mein Kampf* was a published
book after all, but that doesn't mean that books themselves are a flawed
technology that those in education should disengage from. But rather,
the examples above highlight that technology has often negative social
consequences, and so the argument that technology is neutral is naïve
at best. This emphasizes the social responsibility of educators both
in reinforcing the position of technology and in exposing students to
potentially harmful environments.

The final strand of this analysis of ed tech criticality comes from
Mike Caulfield (2016). He acknowledged the positive impact of the web
and related technologies but argued that "to do justice to the possibilities means we must take the downsides of these environments seriously
and address them" (para. 7). He adopted the term "digital polarization"

to capture how online technologies lead to increasingly extreme and divided groups. This is evident in trends such as:

Algorithmic filters — These control what the user sees on social media, with the effect of limiting exposure to opinions different than our own.

Misinformation and "fake news" — These deliberately seek to reinforce the user's existing worldview and can create "an entirely separate factual universe to its readers."

Harassment, trolling, and "callout culture" on social media — These have the intention and impact of silencing minority voices and opinions.

Organized (sometimes by foreign states) hacking campaigns and bot programs — These seek to fuel distrust, grow conspiracy theories, and undermine democratic institutions.

Caulfield (2017b) gave a telling example of this process in action, demonstrating that, on the social media site Pinterest, a user might find that they go from searching for recipes to anti-vaccination conspiracy theories suggested by the site's algorithms. Within a few clicks, their page has transformed from one filled with recipes for watermelon drinks, say, to one dominated by memes on vaccination conspiracy theories. To the unwitting user, the presentation of such content gives it credibility and normality that it does not warrant. And of course, from here the algorithms promote further content on government plots, antisemitic theories of a secret world order, and so on. This highlights one of the significant shifts that has occurred since the advent of the early technologies we have covered in this book, such as the web browser, wikis, and blogs, around the discoverability of content. Previously, discovering online content required an active effort from the user to follow suggestions from blog rolls, undertake searches, click on links, and so on.

When these technologies removed the publication filter that had existed hitherto, it was entirely predictable that along with the new release and useful, humorous, informative content would come undesirable content. However, it required an active, cognitive choice to seek this out, which meant that its impact on wider society was limited. What the type of algorithmic-driven approach that Caulfield highlighted does is to transform discovery into a passive rather than an active process. This opens up a whole new audience for racist, misogynistic, and conspiracy theory sites, and this passive presentation helps to normalize these views. If they're presented regularly and alongside reputable news sources, then they begin to take on legitimacy for people who lack the critical abilities and information networks to see through them and to contradict them.

What Gilliard (2017), Watters (2018b), and Caulfield (2016, 2017b) each provide through these three strands of ed tech critique are aspects of what we can term "the dark side of ed tech." These can be summarized as issues of privacy and data intrusion, social impact, and digital polarization. Taking on these challenges provides a framework for how those involved in ed tech can proceed. Doing so incorporates four elements that acknowledge the dark side of ed tech, without resolving to abandon the use of all technology in an educational context. These four approaches have an increasing level of effort and expertise but are applicable for most educators.

The first element is that of responsibility or duty of care. As educators, it is important to acknowledge the type of negative aspects set out above, and not to unknowingly commit students to the use of technologies or approaches that can lead to invasion of privacy or polarization. Higher education operates within society, and so has a role in both shaping how the communities use such technology and in holding technology companies to account.

The second element is related to this and can be termed "appropriate skepticism." Educators have the appropriate critical skills to question the claims in technology press releases and media reports. This does not entail rejecting all technology but rather having a healthy, questioning approach to claims regarding the impact of technology.

The third element is to take both of the preceding elements and use them to actively develop skills in students so they can recognize and deal with these issues. For instance, Caulfield (2017a) developed a free, open, online textbook that educators can use to develop these critical skills in students. He based this approach around four moves:

Check for previous work — Look around to see if someone else has already fact-checked the claim or provided a synthesis of research.

Go upstream to the source — Most web content is not original. Go to the original source of the claim to understand the trustworthiness of the information.

Read laterally — Once you get to the source of a claim, read what other people say about the source (publication, author, etc.). The truth is in the network.

Circle back — If you get lost, hit dead ends, or find yourself going down an increasingly confusing rabbit hole, back up and start over. Knowing what you know now, you're likely to take a more informed path with different search terms and better decisions.

This type of activity can be implemented in all subjects and has the advantage of being useful for the study of the topic itself, rather than a separate and often dry "digital competence" type of activity.

The fourth element is to engage in research and evaluation or practice that counters the dark side of tech. The response by academics to any social development is to engage in research and gather evidence. Whether this is addressing the claims of technology, investigating how algorithms shape behaviour, or developing tools that counteract some of the negative aspects, there is a need for universities and research funders to bring critical, research-based approaches to much of ed tech. Golumbia and Gilliard (2018) highlighted examples where resistance to invasive uses of technology has prevented their development, such as the backlash against the Peeple app, which allowed users to give people a rating without their consent. These examples indicate that the negative implementation of technology is not inevitable and that educators can play a role in facilitating these acts of resistance through education, evidence, and analysis.

Ed tech research, then, has begun to witness a shift from straight-forward advocacy, which tended to promote the use of new technologies, to a more critical perspective. This can be framed as a dystopian turn if, for instance, we consider the early technologies in this book — the web, constructivism, wikis, CMC, OER — and associated literature, often marked by exploration of the possibilities of rethinking education in terms of social justice and radical, student-centred visions of education. Compared with the later chapters in the book which look at AI, learning analytics, MOOC, and blockchain — while there are certainly advocates of these technologies for improving the learning experience — the accompanying literature also contains issues relating to privacy, ethics, surveillance, and de-professionalization. If the early years covered in this book were characterized by excitement and hope, the later entries are marked by concern, debate, and anxiety.

There is still insufficient critical thought in much of the ed tech field, but arguably the year 2018 marks a more widespread and receptive approach to critical perspectives. If the evangelist and skeptic approaches represent two distinct groups, then sitting in-between these two is the group most focused on ed tech — the practitioners in universities, schools, and colleges who want to do the best for their learners, and finding a means to navigate this landscape is an important function of that role.

A dystopian turn

YEARS
LATER

BRYANMATHERS

Reclaiming Ed Tech

Having surveyed one particular take on 25 years of ed tech, it is now possible to synthesize some generalities. In this chapter, several themes arising from the analysis of this history will be proposed, and then some suggestions regarding what this means for the next 25 years of ed tech will be proffered.

The first of the general themes is that in ed tech, the *tech* part of the phrase "walks taller." Throughout this book, most of the innovations that appear are technologies. Sometimes these are underpinned with strong accompanying educational frameworks, such as the original CMOOC, but also there are cases of a technology seeking an application, as seen with blockchain. The prominence of technology is undoubtedly a function of the time span of the book, which covers the early phases of the digital revolution. A set of ed tech developments 25 years from now may be better balanced with conceptual frameworks, pedagogies, and social movements. The initial few chapters were, in effect, putting into place the technical infrastructure that would facilitate the ed tech developments to come. The web, CMC, e-learning, wikis, blogs, and so on, can be seen as fundamental tools that allowed the social and educational aspects, both positive and negative, to develop. Thus, the initial focus in this book is on the enabling technologies, but as the chapters progress, the focus is increasingly on the impact of these.

A corollary of this is that some of the innocence and optimism invested in new technologies is no longer a valid stance, as chapter 25 highlighted. In each of the technologies, from the web to analytics, there are negative social consequences. There is sufficient experience of these now to predict at least some of these undesirable outcomes. Their possibility, even inevitability, is not necessarily a reason to refuse to engage with any technology. For example, blogs provide as many, if not more, positive examples as they do negative ones. It is in the nature of an open, unfiltered system that people will publish content many find disagreeable (although not outside of existing laws on defamation, threats, and the incitement of hatred). But these negative consequences are not unexpected or unknowable.

Algorithms shape behaviour, and in the seeds of each technology lies the possibility for future dystopian outcomes. For example, Harwell (2018) discussed the spread of "deepfake" videos, where a video can be created by gathering some facial images (such as those posted on social media) and pasting them onto an existing video. This has led to the weaponization of this technology by misogynists to create realistic fake pornography videos of women they seek to undermine, harass, or humiliate. This use of the technology is entirely (and sadly) predictable, and the claim that technology is neutral is not really sustainable. Harwell quoted Hany Farid, a Dartmouth College computer-science professor who specializes in examining manipulated photos and videos who put it in terms of an analogy:

> If a biologist said, 'Here's a really cool virus; let's see what happens when the public gets their hands on it,' that would not be acceptable. And yet it's what Silicon Valley does all the time," he said. "It's indicative of a very immature industry. We have to understand the harm and slow down on how we deploy technology like this. ("Identity Theft," para. 5)

Therefore, although technology has been the dominant force in ed tech, its prevalence in society now means that the educational component needs to come to the fore.

A second theme is that we see ideas recurring, sometimes with increasing success in their adoption. For example, learning objects were the first attempt at making teaching content reusable, and even though they weren't successful, the ideas they generated led to OER, which begat open textbooks. Partly this is a result of historical amnesia, which I cited as one of the motivations for writing this book. If there is no shared history, then there is a tendency, seen repeatedly over these 25 years, for ideas to be rediscovered. A consequence of this is that it sees every development as operating in isolation instead of building on the theoretical, financial, and administrative research of previous work. In examining the different subcommunities that have evolved under the broad heading of "open education" Weller, Jordan, DeVries, and Rolfe (2018), using a citation analysis method, discovered eight distinct communities. The published papers in these areas rarely cross over and reference work from other communities, which is symptomatic of the year-zero mentality. This is also reinforced by the commercial pressures of ed tech start-ups to position themselves as revolutionary and ground-breaking, and particularly "disruptive" as this promises a sector-wide monopoly.

The recurrence of ideas is also a result of what we might term "techno-optimism" — the belief that "this time it really will work." This can be a consequence of overenthusiastic initial claims, which the technology then takes 10 years or so to realize. For example, while intelligent tutoring systems were woefully inadequate for the claims made for them in the 1980s and 1990s, some of that is justifiable in 2018 (although, equally, some of the claims are still overblown). It is also the case that, conceptually, an idea needs several iterations before it is widely accepted. This is influenced by changes in social attitudes towards the use of technology. When mobile learning required specialist devices or relied on text-based quizzes, its uptake was limited, but the arrival and widespread usage of smartphones and apps fundamentally altered the relation of people to learning in different contexts. The shift has become one of push to pull, from providers trying to encourage learners to use mobile learning approaches to learners expecting it.

A consequence of this iterative approach is that those who have been in the ed tech field for a while should be wary of dismissing an idea by saying "We tried that—it didn't work." Virtual reality and immersive worlds may be a good example of this, the first attempts typified by Second Life failed to realize the claims made for it, but there have been sufficient changes since then to make versions of this a viable ed tech, particularly in specific domains. Technology and attitudes can change quietly, and what seemed difficult five years ago is now feasible. Conversely, for those proposing a new idea, there is a need to understand why previous attempts failed and to learn from that experience. This is not to suggest that all ideas will inevitably succeed; some of the claims made for AI, for example, are as far-fetched (and as undesirable) now as they were in the 1980s.

A third emergent theme is how technology outside of education has consistently been co-opted for educational purposes. This has met with varying degrees of success. Blogs, for instance, are an ideal educational technology, whereas blockchain has something of the air of a technology in search of an educational application. The popularity of—or the number of *Wired* headlines about—a technology does not automatically make it a contender as a useful technology for education. More subtly, this adoption means that technology which has not been designed specifically for education is deployed in a context where some requirements may be different. For instance, the adoption of Facebook to create course-specific groups that are a formal component of study—i.e., students cannot complete their studies, or are severely disadvantaged, if they do not use it—provides both benefits and challenges for an educator. It immediately provides a well-structured platform with many desirable tools and features and is one that is familiar to many students.

This can effectively encourage dialogue since the initial barrier to technology adoption is lessened—students don't need to learn or remember to go to a new platform. This means the type of conversations an educator may wish to encourage can be boot-strapped and may start earlier. However, as we have covered elsewhere, the use of commercial social media platforms, such as Facebook, carries several issues, including privacy, data surveillance, and the forcing of students onto a platform they may have consciously chosen to avoid. The convenience of the third-party choice is heavily compromised by it not being a technology designed specifically for educational purposes.

In a global survey of universities, Orr, Weller, and Farrow (2018) reported that the technologies that are most widely adopted and deeply embedded in higher education institutions tend to correlate closely with core university functions, which are broadly categorized as content, delivery, and recognition (Agarwal, 2016). For example, OER, LMS, and e-portfolios from the selection in this book are all widely deployed, and these types of technology relate very closely to these core functions. They are also technologies designed specifically for education, even if their roots can be found in other technologies.

This preference for technologies that are education-specific emphasizes that higher education is a complex, highly interdependent system. It is not like the banking, music, or media industries; rather, while it has some similarities with those sectors, it has many more differences. The simple transfer of technology from other sectors often fails to appreciate the socio-cultural context in which education operates. Generally, only those technologies that directly offer an improved, or alternative, means of addressing the core functions of education achieve widespread adoption.

The cautious adoption of technology can be seen as a further theme. Contrary to some of the rhetoric about higher education's inability to change, the coverage in this book highlights that innovation does indeed arise frequently and across a wide range of educational contexts. Taken as a whole, this review of the last 25 years in ed tech reveals a rich history of innovation: MOOC, Web 2.0, BBS, PLE, connectivism — these all saw periods of exciting innovation and, even if they were not always successful, they posed fundamental questions regarding what education is for and how best to realize it. Accusations that education is fundamentally unchanged from 100 years ago (e.g., Parr, 2012) are mistaken and demonstrate a lack of knowledge about the sector.

However, it is also true that change is not always rapid. One of the complaints, particularly from outsiders, is that higher education is resistant, and slow, to change. This is true, but this can also be framed as a strength. Universities have been around longer than Google, after all, and part of their appeal is their longevity. This entails a certain conservatism regarding current trends, so as institutions they resist abandoning all existing practice in favour of the latest technology.

Libraries weren't closed and replaced with LaserDiscs in the 1990s, partly because the timeframes that universities operate over are longer (and because it would have been a bad idea). This is one of the major, and often misunderstood, differences between higher education and the other sectors that it is frequently implored to learn from — they are operating over different frequencies.

The language of start-ups and technology companies pervades much of the ed tech world, but these phrases are used in very different contexts. Unless a university principal is being required to save a university from imminent collapse, the kind of high-pressure, rapid institutional transformation often seen in tech companies is disruptive (in its original sense) and harmful to the functioning of a university. Universities operate over long timeframes and have often existed for over 50 or 100 years. Their very function is based on their longevity and adherence to core principles rather than rapid changes and then obsolescence. This is perhaps analogous to different sound frequencies. Universities operate like a low-frequency sound, such as a bass drum, whereas technology companies are a high-frequency sound, like a whistle. Over the same time period, there will be waves in both, but far more peaks and troughs will occur in the high-frequency one. Ed tech, then, is operating in a fundamentally different context to other tech companies, and this is perfectly valid and appropriate. Ed tech is not a game for the impatient.

An underlying factor for some of this dissonance is the dominance of the disruption theory we encountered in various places throughout this history (Christensen, 1997). The original application of the term was a useful means of framing how digital technology could create new markets and overtake existing ones, the way digital photography, say, disrupted the traditional camera market. However, it has acquired the status of myth in the technology industry (Watters, 2013a), to the extent that it is both a specified aim compared with an unintended outcome, and indeed is the only desirable outcome for many investments. It is a term frequently associated with ed tech or with innovators to emphasize their independence from the conventional modes of working. For instance, Richard Branson organized an event labelled "Disruptors 2015 — The Future of Education: Does the Current Model Make the

Grade?" (Virgin.com, 2015), which featured many ed tech start-ups but few academics or universities.

What the above consideration of different frequencies illustrates is that, given its dominance in much of ed tech discourse, disruption is simply not a very useful theory to apply to the education sector. One of the defining characteristics of higher education is its longevity, while disruption theory relies on the destruction of a sector. Even if we accept that disruption does occur elsewhere, although this is refuted by many (Dvorak, 2004), it is an inappropriate model or explanation to apply to higher education, like using a description of changes at the cellular level to explain a psychological phenomenon — it might be inveigled in to service, but it is not an effective means of predicting, describing, modelling, or adjusting. There are lots of other reasons to be skeptical of those who promote the idea of disruption, but in higher education, at least, it is simply not a very productive tool to work with.

Phipps (2018) reveals how ed tech vendors seek to ensure that academics are absent when they are pitching technology solutions to universities. He states that vendors "don't want any academics that might end up as users in that room asking difficult questions" (para. 12). Partly this is because vendors will often use powerful but largely meaningless and discredited theories, such as disruption, digital natives, and learning styles. These theories can be effective in creating a narrative of a need for urgent change, underwritten by the Darwinian survival ethos we encountered at the start of this book. However, as I hope this book indicates, an analysis of these motivating factors usually undermines their authority. There is a distinct need for educational technologists to be "in the room" for such pitches, then, and to have an appreciation of both the possible benefits of any technology and the limitations of the associated promises and threats.

The absence of the human impact in much of the discourse around disruption leads to the final theme arising from analysis of the past 25 years, which can be thought of as the role of people in ed tech. Much of the technology covered in these chapters can be seen as representing two distinct ideologies: those that help the educator or those that replace them. Technologies such as wikis, OER, CMC, blogs, and even Second Life have, as their primary aim to find technology that can enhance education, either for a new set of learners, to realize new approaches, or sometimes, just to experiment. Other approaches are oftentimes framed in terms of removing human educators in a bid for improved efficiency and scale: AI, learning analytics, or MOOC. This is not ubiquitous across their associated literature; for example, learning analytics can be used to help human educators better support learners. But often the hype and associated interest is around the large-scale implementation of automated learning. Higher education is most successful when it is framed as a human enterprise, and the technology that is likely to be both impactful and culturally beneficial is that which recognizes this and seeks to work collaboratively with human educators.

This human aspect is also a key component for consideration of the technologies or approaches that are successful. As seen with developments such as e-learning standards and learning objects, a prohibitive factor for adoption is the return on effort. If an educational technology requires excessive effort for low perceived reward, then it will usually fail, or at least require another iteration to be successful. This is the case even if the long-term goal would be beneficial; educators operate in a time-constrained present and need an identifiable benefit. This return on investment paradox is one area where funding from national agencies can be useful in overcoming the initial impetus required to reach a level where the benefits can be identified. Similarly, ed tech exists as part of a socio-cultural system that is decidedly human. For instance, many of the requirements for the successful implementation of e-portfolios and digital badges are not related to the technology, but rather to how people will recognize, use, and, ultimately, require them.

When we look back over the last 25 years, the picture that emerges is a mixed one. Clearly, a considerable shift in higher education practice has taken place, driven by technology adoption. Yet, at the same time, nothing much has changed, and many ed tech developments have failed to have a significant impact. "Everything changes while simultaneously remaining the same," is perhaps the rather paradoxical conclusion. Accepting this as the framework within which ed tech operates, rather than either extreme, however, is a good piece of advice for anyone entering into this field. And the best way to negotiate this paradox is by understanding the recent history that makes it the case.

This paradox of change and seeming unchanging nature has an analogy with books and reading. If you were to look at reading 25 years ago and today, then superficially, nothing much has changed — the classic image is of someone reading a hardback book in quiet solitude. And yet, it doesn't take much examination to appreciate just how wholly different the context is within which that reading occurs. In terms of technology, there is an abundance of audiobooks and e-books; retail occurs largely through online providers, such as Amazon; publishing has seen a rapid growth in self-publishing and crowdfunding models; and the writing of books sees extensive use of blogs, fan fiction, online research and dissemination that occurs through social media and accompanying material found online. The business of books and the society within which books exist is almost unrecognizable from 25 years ago.

So how to reconcile these two elements of seeming resistance to change and yet large-scale innovation? I would suggest that both books and education have what might be termed a "core of immutability" — that is, there is some aspect at their core that does not alter. Indeed, this essence is part of the reason we hold them in high social value: they echo back through history and evoke generally positive emotions. This core is, for both of them, around the individual focus on a task that is conducted largely in the mind — the indulgence in what is essentially a cognitive art form. They are both fundamentally human: maybe AI can write passable books in the future, and maybe it can provide a reasonable level of learner support, but AI is a long way from capturing that human element of flexibility and creativity that are deeply embedded in books and education and that are a part of their appeal.

Inevitably, any analysis of recent history leads to some conjecture about the future. I will resist a "25 Years in the future of ed tech" conclusion, however, because predicting the future of education is a game to which we never seem to learn the rules. Extrapolating from the themes above, some of the following rules about considering the future can nonetheless be deduced and associated with some general predictions.

The first rule to learn about change in higher education is that, as we have just seen, very little changes while simultaneously everything changes. Therefore, any prediction that highlights just one of these elements underestimates either the core of immutability of the general higher education system or the degree of innovation that occurs within it. So, a prediction would be that the future of education will look not dissimilar on the surface, but closer inspection will reveal significant changes around the use of technology to support learning.

A second rule is that technological change is rarely about the technologies, as discussed above with innovations such as e-portfolios or digital badges. The technologies may be fairly robust and straight-forward, but what they require in order to have an impact is a shift in cultural attitudes from employers and learners regarding recognition, the format of learning, and alternative accreditation. A second predic-tion, then, will be that many existing technologies will still be around, but some of them will have developed the appropriate social structures for broad adoption, whereas others will have withered in face of this task.

The third rule is to recognize the historical amnesia in much of educational technology that this book has highlighted, which arises from people entering the field from elsewhere and from ed tech vendors deliberately seeking to position a technology as new and revolutionary. A related prediction, then, will be that exactly the same technologies we see now will be present in the future, but under different names and with some variations.

The fourth and final rule I would suggest is that, as chapter 25 argued, technology is not ethically or politically neutral. This becomes increasingly significant as technology continues to affect all aspects of society. The prediction here, then, is that awareness of this will continue to grow, with educators and learners viewing technology use in education as much as a political choice as it is an educational one. The development of new technologies will be couched not just in the language of technology but also in terms of political and socio-logical impact. Ed tech practitioners who ignore these factors may well find themselves trying to explain the negative interpretations of their approach before it has started.

Some aspects in the future use of ed tech will become common-place as a trajectory of what we have now. For instance, the use of online education will expand as people are increasingly comfortable and adept at operating online. The distinction between face-to-face and online will continue to diminish, such that all university study will be, to an extent, blended. The use of narrow AI focused on particular tasks will increase, but so too will the skepticism around what this means. Similarly, data-driven approaches such as learning analytics will become an increasingly contested ground, between what is possible, what is ethical, what is desirable from a learner perspective, and what is useful for an educator.

In short, the future of ed tech will resemble the present situation pretty closely but with the role of technology becoming ever more pervasive in the educational process. If it is not already true, then in 25 years it certainly will be, that all learning is technology-enhanced learning. This establishes an onus on educators, universities, and learners themselves to critically reflect on the role of that technology. The future of ed tech, then, is likely to be one where the relationship between people and increasingly powerful technology is one that is constantly examined and negotiated. We will probably not see any grand revolution in the higher education space, so don't expect the type of future often predicted by educational technology entrepreneurs, wherein all existing universities are made redundant by a new technology-centric model. Instead, we will see a continual model of innovation, testing, adaption, and revisiting within the constraints of an existing and robust system. And hopefully, that model will be one that acknowledges, learns from, and remembers its history.

REFERENCES

Abramovich, S., Schunn, C., & Higashi, R. M. (2013). Are badges useful in education? It depends upon the type of badge and expertise of learner. *Educational Technology Research and Development, 61*(2), 217–232. https://doi.org/10.1007/s11423-013-9289-2

Agarwal, A. (2016, May 12). Where higher education is headed in the 21st century: Unbundling the clock, curriculum, and credential. *The Times of India.* Retrieved from https://timesofindia.indiatimes.com/blogs/toi-edit-page/where-higher-education-is-headed-in-the-21st-century-unbundling-the-clock-curriculum-and-credential/

Agnihotri, L., & Ott, A. (2014). Building a student at-risk model: An end-to-end perspective from user to data scientist. In J. Stamper, Z. Pardos, M. Mavrikis, & B. M. McLaren (Eds.), *Educational data mining 2014: Proceedings of the 7th international conference on educational data mining* (pp. 209–212). London, UK: Institute of Education. Retrieved from http://educationaldatamining.org/EDM2014/uploads/procs2014/short%20papers/209_EDM-2014-Short.pdf

Alexander, B. (2006). Web 2.0: A new wave of innovation for teaching and learning? *EDUCAUSE Review, 41*(2), 32–44. Retrieved from https://er.educause.edu/articles/2006/1/web-20-a-new-wave-of-innovation-for-teaching-and-learning

Allen, F. E. (2011, October 21). Disneyland uses "electronic whip" on employees. *Forbes.* Retrieved from https://www.forbes.com/sites/frederickallen/2011/10/21/disneyland-uses-electronic-whip-on-employees/

Almeida, N. (2017). Open educational resources and rhetorical paradox in the neoliberal univers(ity). *Journal of Critical Library and Information Studies* 1. https://doi.org/10.24242/jclis.v1i1.16

Ambrose, G., Anthony, E., & Clark, G. (2016, November 13). Digital badging in the MOOC space. *EDUCAUSE Review.* Retrieved from https://er.educause.edu/articles/2016/11/digital-badging-in-the-mooc-space

Anderson, A., Huttenlocher, D., Kleinberg, J., & Leskovec, J. (2013). Steering user behavior with badges. In *Proceedings of the 22nd International Conference on World Wide Web* (pp. 95–106). New York, NY: Association for Computing Machinery.

Anderson, J. R., Boyle, C. F., & Reiser, B. J. (1985). Intelligent tutoring systems. *Science, 228*(4698), 456–462. https://doi.org/10.1126/science.228.4698.456

Arnold, K. E., & Pistilli, M. D. (2012). Course signals at Purdue: Using learning analytics to increase student success. In S. Buckingham Shum, D. Gasevic, & R. Ferguson (Eds.), *Proceedings of the 2nd International Conference on Learning Analytics and Knowledge* (pp. 267–270). New York, NY: Association for Computing Machinery.

Astleitner, H. (2000). A review of motivational and emotional strategies to reduce dropout in web-based distance education. In D. Leutner & R. Brünken (Eds.), *Neue Medien in Unterricht, Aus- und Weiterbildung* [New media in education, training and further education] (pp. 17–24). Munich, Germany: Waxmann.

Attwell, G. (2007). Personal learning environments — the future of eLearning? *elearning Papers, 2*(1), 1–8. Retrieved from http://digtechitalia.pbworks.com/w/file/fetch/88358195/Atwell%202007.pdf

Bacon, S., & Dillon, T. (2006). *The potential of open source approaches for education.* Bristol, UK: FutureLab. Retrieved from https://www.nfer.ac.uk/media/1821/futl58.pdf

Bailey, S. (2015, July). Skipping church? Facial recognition software could be tracking you. *The Washington Post.* Retrieved from https://www.washingtonpost.com/news/acts-of-faith/wp/2015/07/24/skipping-church-facial-recognition-software-could-be-tracking-you/

Baker, S. C., Wentz, R. K., & Woods, M. M. (2009). Using virtual worlds in education: Second Life® as an educational tool. *Teaching of Psychology, 36*(1), 59–64. https://doi.org/10.1080/00986280802529079

Barber, M., Donnelly, K., & Rizvi, S. (2013). An avalanche is coming: Higher education and the revolution ahead. London, UK: Institute for Public Policy Research. Retrieved from https://www.ippr.org/publications/an-avalanche-is-coming-higher-education-and-the-revolution-ahead

Barrows H., & Tamblyn R. (Eds.). (1980). *Problem-based learning: An approach to medical education.* New York, NY: Springer.

Bates, A. W. (1995). *Technology, open learning and distance education.* London: Routledge.

Batson, T. (2002, November). The electronic portfolio boom: What's it all about? *CampusTechnology.* Retrieved from https://campustechnology.com/articles/2002/11/the-electronic-portfolio-boom-whats-it-all-about.aspx

BCcampus. (2019). Open textbook stats [Website content]. Retrieved from https://open.bccampus.ca/advocate-for-open-education/open-textbook-stats/

Beetham, H. (2005). E-portfolios in post-16 learning in the UK: Developments, issues and opportunities. Retrieved from http://bectaepexpert.pbworks.com/f/Beetham+eportfolio_ped.doc

Bennett, L. (2018). *Students' learning responses to receiving dashboard data* (Society for Research into Higher Education Report). Retrieved from https://www.srhe.ac.uk/downloads/reports-2016/LizBennet-scoping2016.pdf

Benton, R. (1996). Making the medium the message: Using an electronic bulletin board system for promoting and revitalizing Māori. In M. Warschauer (Ed.), *Telecollaboration in foreign language learning: Proceedings of the Hawai'i Symposium* (pp. 187–204). Honolulu, Hawai'i: University of Hawai'i Press.

Berners-Lee, T.J. (n.d.). What made you think of the WWW? *Answers for young people.* Retrieved from https://www.w3.org/People/Berners-Lee/Kids.html#What

Berners-Lee, T.J. (1989). Information management: A proposal. (CERN Report No. CERN-DD-89-001-OC). Retrieved from https://www.w3.org/History/1989/proposal.html

Bliss, T.J., Hilton, J., Wiley, D., & Thanos, K. (2013). The cost and quality of online open textbooks: Perceptions of community college faculty and students. *First Monday, 18*(1). https://doi.org/10.5210/fm.v18i1.3972

Bodily, R., Nyland, R., & Wiley, D. (2017). The RISE framework: Using learning analytics to automatically identify open educational resources for continuous improvement. *The International Review of Research in Open and Distributed Learning, 18*(2). https://doi.org/10.19173/irrodl.v18i2.2952

Bork, A., & Britton Jr., D.R. (1998). The web is not yet suitable for learning. *Computer. 31*(6), 115–116. https://doi.org/10.1109/2.683015

Brandman University. (2015, January 10). Brandman University teams up with Credly to issue digital badges as part of competency-based education degrees. *Brandman News.* Retrieved from https://www.brandman.edu/news-and-events/news/brandman-university-teams-up-with-credly-to-issue-digital-badges-as-part-of-competencybased-educatio

Bruner, J.S. (1978). The role of dialogue in language acquisition. In A. Sinclair, R.J. Jarvelle, & W.J.M. Levelt (Eds.), *The child's concept of language* (pp. 241–255). New York, NY: Springer-Verlag.

Burg, J., Murphy, C., & Pétraud, J. (2018). Blockchain for international development: Using a learning agenda to address knowledge gaps [Blog post]. *MERL Tech.* Retrieved from http://merltech.org/blockchain-for-international-development-using-a-learning-agenda-to-address-knowledge-gaps/

Bush, V. (1945). As we may think. *The Atlantic Monthly, 176*(1), 101–108.

Cadwalldr, C., & Graham-Harrison. E. (2018, March 17). Revealed: 50 million Facebook profiles harvested for Cambridge Analytica in major data breach. *The Guardian.* Retrieved from https://www.theguardian.com/news/2018/mar/17/cambridge-analytica-facebook-influence-us-election

Carr-Chellman, A., & Duchastel, P. (2000). The ideal online course. *British Journal of Educational Technology, 31*(3), 229–241. https://doi.org/10.1111/1467-8535.00154

Caulfield, M. (2013a, May 30). As we were saying... (Coursera as provider of courseware) [Blog post]. *Hapgood.* Retrieved from https://hapgood.us/2013/05/30/as-we-were-saying-coursera-as-provider-of-courseware/

Caulfield, M. (2013b, September 26). A simple, less mathematical way to understand the course signals issue [Blog post]. *Hapgood.* Retrieved from https://hapgood.us/2013/09/26/a-simple-less-mathematical-way-to-understand-the-course-signals-issue/

Caulfield, M. (2016, December 7). Announcing the digital polarization initiative, an open pedagogy project [Blog post]. *Hapgood.* Retrieved from https://hapgood.us/2016/12/07/announcing-the-digital-polarization-initiative-an-open-pedagogy-joint/

Caulfield, M. (2017a). *Web literacy for student fact checkers ... and other people who care about facts*. Retrieved from https://webliteracy.pressbooks.com/

Caulfield, M. (2017b, November). Digital polarization on Pinterest is scary aggressive [Blog post]. *Hapgood*. Retrieved from https://hapgood.us/2017/11/13/digital-polarization-on-pinterest-is-scary-aggressive/

Cellan-Jones, R. (2018, October 2). Could Blockchain solve Irish border issue? *BBC News*, Retrieved from https://www.bbc.co.uk/news/technology-45725572

Chatham-Carpenter, A., Seawel, L., & Raschig, J. (2010). Avoiding the pitfalls: Current practices and recommendations for ePortfolios in higher education. *Journal of Educational Technology Systems, 38*(4), 437–456. https://doi.org/10.2190/ET.38.4.e

Chi, M. T., Glaser, R., & Farr, M. J. (Eds.). (2014). *The nature of expertise*. New York, NY: Psychology Press.

Christenson, C. (1997). *The innovator's dilemma*. Cambridge, MA: Harvard Business School Press.

Christensen, C. M., Horn, M. B., Caldera, L., & Soares, L. (2011). *Disrupting college: How disruptive innovation can deliver quality and affordability to postsecondary education* (Innosight Institute Report). Retrieved from https://files.eric.ed.gov/fulltext/ED535182.pdf

Christensen, G., Steinmetz, A., Alcorn, B., Bennett, A., Woods, D., & Emanuel, E. (2013). *The MOOC phenomenon: Who takes massive open online courses and why?* http://dx.doi.org/10.2139/ssrn.2350964

Clarke, M. (2010). New art history. In *The Concise Oxford Dictionary of Art Terms*. Oxford, UK: Oxford University Press. Retrieved from https://www.oxfordreference.com/view/10.1093/acref/9780199569922.001.0001/acref-9780199569922-e-1164?rskey=273PK9&result=1

Clay, J. (2009, September 9). The VLE is dead–The movie [Video file]. Retrieved from http://elearningstuff.net/2009/09/09/the-vle-is-dead-the-movie/

Clow, D. (2011, February 28). The learning analytics cycle [Blog post]. Retrieved from https://dougclow.org/2011/02/28/the-learning-analytics-cycle/

Clow, D. (2013, December 20). The numbers are people [Blog post]. Retrieved from https://dougclow.org/2013/12/20/the-numbers-are-people/

Conole, G., de Laat, M., Dillon, T., & Darby, J. (2008). "Disruptive technologies," "pedagogical innovation": What's new? Findings from an in-depth study of students' use and perception of technology. *Computers and Education, 50*, 511–524. https://doi.org/10.1016/j.compedu.2007.09.009

Constantinides, E., & Zinck Stagno, M. C. (2011). Potential of the social media as instruments of higher education marketing: A segmentation study. *Journal of Marketing for Higher Education, 21*(1), 7–24. https://doi.org/10.1080/08841241.2011.573593

Corbett, A. T., Koedinger, K. R., & Anderson, J. R. (1997). Intelligent tutoring systems. In M. G. Helander, T. K. Landauer, & P. V. Prabhu (Eds.), *Handbook of human-computer interaction* (2nd ed., pp. 849–874). New York, NY: Elsevier.

Corcoran, B. (2018, December 11). How Google's former China chief thinks AI will reshape teaching. *EdSurge*. Retrieved from https://www.edsurge.com/news/2018-12-11-how-this-famed-chinese-venture-capitalist-thinks-ai-will-reshape-teaching

Cormier, D. (2008a, February 29). Rhizomatic knowledge communities: Edtechtalk [Blog post]. Retrieved from http://davecormier.com/edblog/2008/02/29/rhizomatic-knowledge-communities-edtechtalk-webcast-academy/

Cormier, D. (2008b, June 3). Rhizomatic education : Community as curriculum [Blog post]. Retrieved from http://davecormier.com/edblog/2008/06/03/rhizomatic-education-community-as-curriculum/

Cormier, D. (2014). Rhiz014 — The MOOC that community built. *The International Journal for Innovation and Quality in Learning, 3*, 107–110. Retrieved from https://empower.eadtu.eu/images/fields-of-expertise/OERsMOOCs/INNOQUAL-Issue-3-Publication-Sep-2014-FINAL-w-cover.pdf#page=114

Correll, S. (1995). The ethnography of an electronic bar: The lesbian café. *Journal of Contemporary Ethnography, 24*(3), 270–298. https://doi.org/10.1177/089124195024003002

Costa, C. (2016). Double gamers: Academics between fields. *British Journal of Sociology of Education, 37*(7), 993–1013. http://dx.doi.org/10.1080/01425692.2014.982861

Costa, C. (2013). *The participatory web in the context of academic research: Landscapes of change and conflicts* (Doctoral dissertation). University of Salford.

Coughlan, S. (2016, May 26). Online degree units to cut tuition fees. *BBC News*. Retrieved from https://www.bbc.co.uk/news/education-36378572

Coughlan, S. (2018, March 6). University offers science degree online for £5,650 per year. *BBC News*. Retrieved from https://www.bbc.co.uk/news/education-43288793

Coughlan, T., Pitt, R., & McAndrew, P. (2013). Building open bridges: Collaborative remixing and reuse of open educational resources across organisations. In R. Grinter, T. Rodden, P. Aoki, E. Cutrell, R. Jeffries, & G. Olson (Eds.), *Proceedings of the SIGCHI Conference on Human Factors in Computing Systems* (pp. 991–1000). New York, NY: Association for Computing Machinery.

Coursera. (2013, May 30). 10 US state university systems and public institutions join Coursera to explore MOOC-based learning and collaboration on campus [Blog post]. Retrieved from https://blog.coursera.org/10-us-state-university-systems-and-public/

Creative Commons. (2015). State of the Commons [Website content]. Retrieved from https://stateof.creativecommons.org/2015/

Crowston, K., & Howison, J. (2005). The social structure of free and open source software development. *First Monday, 10*(2). Retrieved from https://firstmonday.org/article/view/1207/1127

Cullen, J., & Bryman, A. (1988). The knowledge acquisition bottleneck: Time for reassessment? *Expert Systems, 5*(3), 216–225. https://doi.org/10.1111/j.1468-0394.1988.tb00065.x

Czerniewicz, L. (2019, March 20). South African decision makers debate project findings. *The Unbundled University*. Retrieved from https://unbundled uni.com/2019/03/20/south-african-decision-makers-debate-project-findings/

Czerniewicz, L. (2018). Unbundling and rebundling higher education in an age of inequality. *EDUCAUSE Review, 53*(6), 10–24. Retrieved from https://er.educause.edu/articles/2018/10/unbundling-and-rebundling-higher-education-in-an-age-of-inequality

Dabbagh, N., & Kitsantas, A. (2012). Personal Learning Environments, social media, and self-regulated learning: A natural formula for connecting formal and informal learning. *The Internet and Higher Education, 15*(1), 3–8. https://doi.org/10.1016/j.iheduc.2011.06.002

Davis, K., & Singh, S. (2015). Digital badges in afterschool learning: Documenting the perspectives and experiences of students and educators. *Computers & Education, 88*, 72–83. https://doi.org/10.1016/j.compedu.2015.04.011

Delaney, P.J., Menzies, V., & Nelson, K.J. (2012). Vlogging campus community stories. Retrieved from https://eprints.qut.edu.au/53698/2/53698.pdf

Deleuze, G., & Guatarri. F. (1987). *A thousand plateaus: Capitalism and schizophrenia* (B Massumi Trans.). Minneapolis, MN: University of Minnesota Press.

de los Arcos, B., Farrow, R., Perryman, L.-A., Pitt, R., & Weller, M. (2014). *OER evidence report 2013–2014: Building understanding of open education*. Milton Keynes, UK: OER Research Hub. Retrieved from https://oerresearchhub.files.wordpress.com/2014/11/oerrh-evidence-report-2014.pdf

De Montfort University (DMU). (2018, February 5). Student vloggers project helps DMU make shortlist for national marketing award. Retrieved from https://www.dmu.ac.uk/dmu-students/hot-topics/2018/february/student-vloggers-project-shortlisted-for-national-marketing-award.aspx

DeRosa, R. (2015, November) Open textbooks? Ugh [Blog post]. Retrieved from http://robinderosa.net/uncategorized/open-textbooks-ugh/

DeRosa, R. (2016, May). My open textbook: Pedagogy and practice [Blog post]. Retrieved from http://robinderosa.net/uncategorized/my-open-textbook-pedagogy-and-practice/

Doss, H. (2014, June 19). Disruptive innovation is nonsense. *Forbes*. Retrieved from https://www.forbes.com/sites/henrydoss/2014/06/19/disruptive-innovation-is-nonsense/#4f082f2622f0

Downes, S. (2001). Learning objects: Resources for distance education worldwide. *The International Review of Research in Open and Distributed Learning, 2*(1). http://dx.doi.org/10.19173/irrodl.v2i1.32

Downes, S., & Siemens, G. (2008). CCK08: The distributed course [Online course: MOOC]. Retrieved from https://sites.google.com/site/themoocguide/3-cck08---the-distributed-course

Downes, S., & Siemens, G. (2009). CCK09: The students teach the course [Online course: MOOC]. Retrieved from https://sites.google.com/site/themoocguide/4-cck09---the-students-teach-the-course

Driscoll, M. (2002, January). Blended learning: Let's get beyond the hype. *E-learning,* *3*(3). Retrieved from https://www.researchgate.net/publication/286029739_Blended_learning_Let's_get_beyond_the_hype

Dublin Core Metadata Initiative. (2003). Dublin core metadata element set, version 1.1: Reference description [Report]. Retrieved from https://www.dublincore.org/specifications/dublin-core/dces/2003-02-04

Duval, E. (2005, March 29). Automatic generation of (LOM) metadata [Blog post]. Retrieved from https://erikduval.wordpress.com/2005/03/29/automatic-generation-of-lom-metadata/

Dvorak, J. (2004, August 17). The myth of disruptive technology. *pc Mag.* Retrieved from http://www.pcmag.com/article2/0,2817,1628049,00.asp.

Educause. (2009). 7 things you should know about personal learning environments. *educause Review.* Retrieved from https://library.educause.edu/resources/2009/5/7-things-you-should-know-about-personal-learning-environments

Elkin-Koren, N. (1994). Copyright law and social dialogue on the information superhighway: The case against copyright liability of bulletin board operators. *Cardozo Arts & Entertainment Law Journal, 13,* 345–411.

ePortfolio Ireland. (2019) What, why and how of ePortfolios [Survey reports]. Retrieved from http://eportfoliohub.ie/index.php/reports/

Eysenbach, G. (2006). Citation advantage of open access articles. *PLoS Biology, 4* (5), e157. https://doi.org/10.1371/journal.pbio.0040157

Fagan, N. (2018, August 14). Universities use blockchain to streamline student services. *EdTech Magazine.* Retrieved from https://edtechmagazine.com/higher/article/2018/08/universities-use-blockchain-streamline-student-services

Farrell, N. (2015, February 1). Developing countries think Facebook is the Internet. *Fudzilla.* Retrieved from https://www.fudzilla.com/news/36984-developing-countries-think-facebook-is-the-internet

Farrow, M., Ward, D.D., Klekociuk, S.Z., & Vickers, J.C. (2017). Building capacity for dementia risk reduction: The preventing dementia mooc. *Alzheimer's & Dementia: The Journal of the Alzheimer's Association, 13*(7), P871–P872. https://doi.org/10.1016/j.jalz.2017.06.1244

Feldstein, M. (2017, November 6). How and why the ims failed with lti 2.0. *e-Literate. Retrieved from* https://eliterate.us/ims-failed-lti-2-0/

Ferenstein, G. (2013, January 15). How California's online education pilot will end college as we know it. *TechCrunch.* Retrieved from https://techcrunch.com/2013/01/15/how-californias-new-online-education-pilot-will-end-college-as-we-know-it/

Finn, J., & Lavitt, M. (1994). Computer-based self-help groups for sexual abuse survivors. *Social Work with Groups, 17*(1–2), 21–46. https://doi.org/10.1300/J009v17n01_03

Fischer, L., Hilton, J., Robinson, T.J., & Wiley, D.A. (2015). A multi-institutional study of the impact of open textbook adoption on the learning outcomes of post-secondary students. *Journal of Computing in Higher Education, 27*(3), 159–172. https://doi.org/10.1007/s12528-015-9101-x

Ford, K. C., Veletsianos, G., & Resta, P. (2014). The structure and characteristics of #PhDChat, an emergent online social network. *Journal of Interactive Media in Education, 2014*(1), Art. 8. http://doi.org/10.5334/2014-08

Fullick, M. (2014, November 6). The times, they are (always) a-changin'. *University Affairs*. Retrieved from https://www.universityaffairs.ca/opinion/speculative-diction/times-always-changin/

Galea-Pace, S. (2019, January 9). University of Bahrain set to become one of first universities to issue digital diplomas anchored to blockchain. *Business Chief*. Retrieved from https://middleeast.businesschief.com/leadership/2246/University-of-Bahrain-set-to-become-one-of-first-universities-to-issue-digital-diplomas-anchored-to-blockchain

Garrett, R. (2004, January 1). The real story behind the failure of U.K. eUniversity. *EDUCAUSE Review*. Retrieved from https://er.educause.edu/articles/2004/1/the-real-story-behind-the-failure-of-uk-euniversity

Gasevic, D., Siemens, G., & Rosé, C. P. (2017). Guest editorial: Special section on learning analytics. *IEEE Transactions on Learning Technologies*, (1), 3–5.

Geist, M. (2006, August 14). Patent battle over teaching tools. *BBC News*. Retrieved from http://news.bbc.co.uk/1/hi/technology/4790485.stm

Gibson, D., Ostashewski, N., Flintoff, K., Grant, S., & Knight, E. (2015). Digital badges in education. *Education and Information Technologies, 20*(2), 403–410. http://dx.doi.org/10.1007/s10639-013-9291-7

Giles, M. W. (1996). From Gutenberg to gigabytes: Scholarly communication in the age of cyberspace. *The Journal of Politics, 58*(3), 613–626.

Gilliard, C. (2017, December 29). One ring doorbell to surveil them all . . . [Tweet]. Retrieved from https://twitter.com/hypervisible/status/946822278582603777

Godin, S. (2016, March 1). Will this be on the test? *The Startup*. Retrieved from https://medium.com/swlh/will-this-be-on-the-test-237ae9cc53b4#.zdksfx36e

Golumbia, D. (2018, March). Zealots of the blockchain. *The Baffler, 38*. Retrieved from https://thebaffler.com/salvos/zealots-of-the-blockchain-golumbia

Golumbia D., & Gilliard, C. (2018, March 9). There are no guardrails on our privacy dystopia. *Motherboard*. Retrieved from https://motherboard.vice.com/en_us/article/zmwaee/there-are-no-guardrails-on-our-privacy-dystopia

Graells-Garrido, E., Lalmas, M., & Menczer, F. (2015). First women, second sex: Gender bias in Wikipedia. In *Proceedings of the 26th ACM conference on hypertext & social media* (pp. 165–174). New York, NY: Association for Computing Machinery. https://doi.org/10.1145/2700171.279106

Grech, A., & Camilleri, A. F. (2017). *Blockchain in education*. Luxembourg: Joint Research Center. Retrieved from https://publications.europa.eu/en/publication-detail/-/publication/fe2e2bc8-c500-11e7-9b01-01aa75ed71a1/language-en

Greene, B. A., & Land, S. M. (2000). A qualitative analysis of scaffolding use in a resource-based learning environment involving the World Wide Web. *Journal of Educational Computing Research, 23*(2), 151–179. http://dx.doi.org/10.2190/1GUB-8UE9-NW80-CQAD

Greene, H., & Crespi, C. (2012). The value of student created videos in the college classroom — an exploratory study in marketing and accounting. *International Journal of Arts & Sciences, 5*(1), 273–283.

Groom, J, (2008a, March 29). Don't call it a blog! [Blog post]. *bavatuedays*. Retrieved from https://bavatuesdays.com/dont-call-it-a-blog/

Groom, J. (2008b, May 7). This ain't yo mama's e-portfolio, part 1. *bavatuesdays*. Retrieved from https://bavatuesdays.com/this-aint-yo-mamas-e-portfolio-part-1/

Groom, J., & Lamb. B. (2014). Reclaiming innovation. *EDUCAUSE Review, 49*(3). Retrieved from https://www.educause.edu/visuals/shared/er/extras/2014/ReclaimingInnovation/default.html

Guzdial, M. (1998). Collaborative websites supporting open authoring. Retrieved from https://www.researchgate.net/profile/Mark_Guzdial/publication/2804108_Collaborative_Websites_Supporting_Open_Authoring/links/5579c99708aeacff2003cb55.pdf

Hadjinicolaou, N. (1978). *Art history and class struggle* (L. Asmal Trans.). London, UK: Pluto.

Harwell, D. (2018, December 30). Fake-porn videos are being weaponized to harass and humiliate women: Everybody is a potential target. *The Washington Post*. Retrieved from https://www.washingtonpost.com/technology/2018/12/30/fake-porn-videos-are-being-weaponized-harass-humiliate-women-everybody-is-potential-target/

Head, Alison J., & Eisenberg, M. B. (2010, March 1). How today's college students use Wikipedia for course-related research. *First Monday, 15*(3). Retrieved from https://journals.uic.edu/ojs/index.php/fm/article/view/2830/2476

Hill, B. M., & Shaw, A. (2013). The Wikipedia gender gap revisited: Characterizing survey response bias with propensity score estimation. *PloS One, 8*(6), e65782. https://doi.org/10.1371/journal.pone.0065782

Hill, K. (2014, October 3). "God view": Uber allegedly stalked users for party-goers' viewing pleasure. *Forbes*. Retrieved from https://www.forbes.com/sites/kashmirhill/2014/10/03/god-view-uber-allegedly-stalked-users-for-party-goers-viewing-pleasure/

Hill, K. (2017, October 11). How Facebook outs sex workers. *Gizmodo*. Retrieved from https://gizmodo.com/how-facebook-outs-sex-workers-1818861596

Hilton, J. (2016). Open educational resources and college textbook choices: a review of research on efficacy and perceptions. *Educational Technology Research and Development, 64*(4), 573–590. https://doi.org/10.1007/s11423-016-9434-9

Hilton III, J., Robinson, T., Wiley, D., & Ackerman, J. (2014). Cost-savings achieved in two semesters through the adoption of open educational resources. *The International Review of Research in Open and Distributed Learning, 15*(2). https://doi.org/10.19173/irrodl.v15i2.1700

Hogan, P. (2015, August 13). We took a tour of the abandoned college campuses of Second Life. *Splinter*. Retrieved from https://splinternews.com/we-took-a-tour-of-the-abandoned-college-campuses-of-sec-1793849944

Hollands, F., & Tirthali, D. (2014). Resource requirements and costs of developing and delivering M O O C s. *The International Review of Research in Open and Distributed Learning, 15*(5). https://doi.org/10.19173/irrodl.v15i5.1901

I M S. (2017). Advancing digital credentials and competency-based learning. *IMS Global Learning Consortium.* Retrieved from https://www.imsglobal.org/initiative/advancing-digital-credentials-and-competency-based-learning

Jackson, A. (2017, September 28). Digital badges are the newest effort to help employees stave off the robots — and major companies are getting onboard. *Business Insider.* Retrieved from https://www.businessinsider.my/ibm-ey-salesforce-digital-badges-certify-employee-skills-2017-9/

Jackson, T. (2018, June 15). Environmental implications of blockchain. *Inside Ecology.* Retrieved from https://insideecology.com/2018/06/15/blockchain-and-the-environment/

James, M. L., Wotring, C. E., & Forrest, E. J. (1995). An exploratory study of the perceived benefits of electronic bulletin board use and their impact on other communication activities. *Journal of Broadcasting & Electronic Media, 39*(1), 30–50. https://doi.org/10.1080/08838159509364287

Jarmon, L., Traphagan, T., Mayrath, M., & Trivedi, A. (2009). Virtual world teaching, experiential learning, and assessment: An interdisciplinary communication course in Second Life. *Computers & Education, 53*(1), 169–182. https://doi.org/10.1016/j.compedu.2009.01.010

Jenkins, H., Purushotma, R., Weigel, M., Clinton, K., & Robison, A. J. (2009). *Confronting the challenges of participatory culture: Media education for the 21st century.* Cambridge, M A : M I T Press.

Jhangiani, R. (2015, November 23). Are open textbooks the end game? [Blog post]. Retrieved from http://thatpsychprof.com/are-open-textbooks-the-end-game/

Jhangiani, R. (2017, January 12). Why have students answer questions when they can write them? [Blog post]. Retrieved from http://thatpsychprof.com/why-have-students-answer-questions-when-they-can-write-them/

Jonassen, D. (1991). Objectivism vs constructivism: Do we need a new philosophical paradigm? *Educational Technology, Research and Development, 39*(3), 5–13.

Jonassen, D., Davidson, M., Collins, M., Campbell, J., & Haag, B. B. (1995). Constructivism and computer-mediated communication in distance education. *American Journal of Distance Education, 9*(2), 7–26. https://doi.org/10.1080/08923649509526885

Jordan, K. (2014). Initial trends in enrolment and completion of massive open online courses. *The International Review of Research in Open and Distributed Learning, 15*(1). https://doi.org/10.19173/irrodl.v15i1.1651

Jordan, K. (2017a). Examining the U K higher education sector through the network of institutional accounts on Twitter. *First Monday, 22*(5). Retrieved from http://firstmonday.org/ojs/index.php/fm/article/view/7133/6145

Jordan, K. (2017b). *Understanding the structure and role of academics' ego-networks on social networking sites* (Doctoral dissertation). The Open University. Retrieved from http://oro.open.ac.uk/48259/

Kemp, J., & Livingstone, D. (2006). Putting a Second Life "metaverse" skin on learning management systems. In D. Livingstone & J. Kemp (Eds.), *Proceedings of the Second Life Education Workshop at the Second Life Community Convention, San Francisco August 20th, 2006* (pp. 13–18). Glasgow, Scotland: The University of Paisley. Retrieved from https://files.eric.ed.gov/fulltext/ED493670.pdf

Kernohan, D. (2014, November 26). Towards a paleoconnectivism reader #opened14 [Blog post]. Retrieved from http://followersoftheapocalyp.se/towards-a-paleoconnectivism-reader-opened14/

King, A. (1993). From sage on the stage to guide on the side. *College Teaching, 41*(1), 30–35. Retrieved from https://doi.org/10.1080/87567555.1993.9926781

Kirriemuir, John. (n.d.). Virtual world watch [Blog post]. Retrieved from http://www.silversprite.com/?page_id=353

Knox, J. (2013). Five critiques of the open educational resources movement. *Teaching in Higher Education, 18*(8), 821–832. https://doi.org/10.1080/13562517.2013.774354

Kop, R. (2011). The challenges to connectivist learning on open online networks: Learning experiences during a massive open online course. *The International Review of Research in Open and Distributed Learning, 12*(3), 19–38. http://dx.doi.org/10.19173/irrodl.v12i3.882

Korn, M. (2014, February 5). Giant résumés fail to impress employers. *Wall Street Journal*. Retrieved from https://www.wsj.com/articles/giant-r233sum233s-fail-to-impress-employers-1391647892

Kortemeyer, G. (2013). Ten years later: Why open educational resources have not noticeably affected higher education, and why we should care. EDUCAUSE *Review, 48*(2). Retrieved from https://er.educause.edu/articles/2013/2/ten-years-later-why-open-educational-resources-have-not-noticeably-affected-higher-education-and-why-we-should-care

Lamb, B. (2018, March 4). An object lesson: My introduction to open. *Mural UDG*. Retrieved from https://muraludg.org/my-introduction-to-open/

Land, R., & Bayne, S. (2005). Screen or monitor? Surveillance and disciplinary power in online learning environments. In R. Land & S. Bayne (Eds.), *Education in cyberspace* (pp. 165–178). London, UK: RoutledgeFalmer.

Lanier, J. (2002). The complexity ceiling. In J. Brockman (Ed.), *The next fifty years: Science in the first half of the twenty-first century* (pp. 216–229). New York, NY: Vintage Press.

Lave, J., & Wenger, E. (1991). *Situated learning: Legitimate peripheral participation.* Cambridge, UK: Cambridge University Press

Law, P. (2015). Digital badging at the Open University: Recognition for informal learning. *Open Learning: The Journal of Open, Distance and e-Learning, 30*(3), 221–234. https://doi.org/10.1080/02680513.2015.1104500

Lawton, W., & Katsomitros, A. (2012). MOOCs and disruptive innovation: The challenge to HE business models. *The Observatory on Borderless Higher Education*. Retrieved from http://www.obhe.ac.uk/documents/view_details?id=929

Learning Wales. (2018). Digital competence framework. Retrieved from https://hwb.gov.wales/draft-curriculum-for-wales-2022/digital-competence-framework-draft-curriculum-for-wales-2022-version

Leckart, S. (2012, March 20). The Stanford education experiment could change higher learning forever. *Wired*. Retrieved from https://www.wired.com/2012/03/ff_aiclass/

Leslie, S. (2012, December 19). Some observations on PLE diagrams [Blog post]. Retrieved from https://scottleslie.ca/edtechpost/wordpress/2012/12/19/ple-diagrams-observations/

Levine, A. (2008, February 15). Re: 25 years of edtech — 1994: Bulletin Board Systems [Blog post]. Retrieved from http://blog.edtechie.net/alt/25-years-of-edtech-1994-bulletin-board-systems/#comment-5035

Levy, S. (2018, November 6). Inside Palmer Luckey's bid to build a border wall. *Wired*. Retrieved from https://www.wired.com/story/palmer-luckey-anduril-border-wall/

Lewin, D. (2013, November 12). After setbacks, online courses are re-thought. *New York Times*. Retrieved from https://www.nytimes.com/2013/12/11/us/after-setbacks-online-courses-are-rethought.html?_r=0

Lorenzo, G., & Ittelson, J. (2005). An overview of e-portfolios. *Educause Learning Initiative*, *1*(1), 1–27. Retrieved from https://library.educause.edu/resources/2005/1/an-overview-of-eportfolios

Lundin, M., Rensfeldt, A. B., Hillman, T., Lantz-Andersson, A., & Peterson, L. (2018). Higher education dominance and siloed knowledge: A systematic review of flipped classroom research. *International Journal of Educational Technology in Higher Education*, *15*(1). https://doi.org/10.1186/s41239-018-0101-6

Lupton, D. (2014). *"Feeling better connected": Academics' use of social media*. Australia: News & Media Research Centre, University of Canberra. Retrieved from https://www.canberra.edu.au/about-uc/faculties/arts-design/attachments2/pdf/n-and-mrc/Feeling-Better-Connected-report-final.pdf

Mackness, J., & Bell, F. (2015). Rhizo14: A rhizomatic learning cMooc in sunlight and in shade. *Open Praxis*, *7*(1), 25–38. Retrieved from https://pdfs.semanticscholar.org/d340/3a4cb4f799c9817e3e299e443a7d3d8cb4f7.pdf

Maher, J., Rooney, K., Toomse-Smith, M., Kiss, Z., Pollard, E., & Williams, M. (2017, June). *Student income and expenditure survey 2014/15: Welsh-domiciled students*. Cardiff, Wales: Department for Business, Innovation and Skills and the Welsh Government.

Manjoo, F. (2009, July 20). Why 2024 will be like nineteen eighty-four. *Slate*. Retrieved from https://slate.com/technology/2009/07/how-amazon-s-remote-deletion-of-e-books-from-the-kindle-paves-the-way-for-book-banning-s-digital-future.html

Marwick, A. E., & boyd, d. (2011). I tweet honestly, I tweet passionately: Twitter users, context collapse, and the imagined audience. *New Media & Society*, *13*(1), 114–133. https://doi.org/10.1177/1461444810365313

Mason, R., & Kaye, A. (Eds.). (1989). *Mindweave: Communication, computers, and distance education*. Oxford, UK: Pergamon Press.

Mason, R., & Rehak, D. (2003). Keeping the learning in learning objects. In A. Littlejohn (Ed.), *Reusing online resources: A sustainable approach to e-learning* (pp. 20–34). London, U K : Kogan Page.

Mayer, R. (2004). Should there be a three-strikes rule against pure discovery learning? The case for guided methods of instruction. *American Psychologist, 59*(1), 14–19. http://dx.doi.org/10.1037/0003-066X.59.1.14

McAvinia, C., & Risquez, A. (2018). Editorial: The #VLEIreland project. *Irish Journal of Technology Enhanced Learning, 3*(2). https://doi.org/10.22554/ijtel.v3i2.37

McDonald, J. (2002). Is "as good as face-to-face" as good as it gets. *Journal of Asynchronous Learning Networks, 6*(2), 10–23. Retrieved from http://www.grandviewcetl.org/wp-content/uploads/2015/10/v6n2_macdonald_1-1.pdf

Mewburn, I., & Thomson, P. (2013). Why do academics blog? An analysis of audiences, purposes and challenges. *Studies in Higher Education, 38*(8), 1105–1119. https://doi.org/10.1080/03075079.2013.835624

Moran, M., Seaman, J., & Tinti-Kane., H. (2011). Teaching, learning, and sharing: How today's higher education faculty use social media. Boston, M A : Pearson Learning Solutions and Babson Survey Research Group.

Morgan, K. (2016, May 24). Moocs prove that universities can and should embrace online learning. *Times Higher Education*. Retrieved from https://www.timeshighereducation.com/blog/moocs-prove-universities-can-and-should-embrace-online-learning

Nelson, L., & Harfield, T. (2017). Giving data meaning: Students should have a say in what analytics tell you about them. *EdSurge*. Retrieved from https://www.edsurge.com/news/2017-08-13-giving-data-meaning-students-should-have-a-say-in-what-analytics-tell-you-about-them

Noam, E. M. (1995). Electronics and the dim future of the university. *Science, 270* (5234), 247–249. Retrieved from https://science.sciencemag.org/content/270/5234/247

Noble, D. F. (1998). Digital diploma mills: The automation of higher education. *Science as Culture, 7*(3), 355–368. https://doi.org/10.1080/09505439809526510

Norman, D. (2008, February 16). On eduglu–part 1: Background [Blog post]. Retrieved from https://darcynorman.net/2008/02/16/on-eduglu-part-1-background/

N Z Q A . (2018, August 1). Micro-credentials system launched. Retrieved from https://www.nzqa.govt.nz/about-us/news/micro-credentials-system-launched/

O E C D . (2005). *E-learning in tertiary education: Where do we stand?* Paris, France: O E C D . Retrieved from https://www.oecd-ilibrary.org/docserver/9789264009219-en.pdf?expires=1566763030&id=id&accname=guest&checksum=4BD037CA011C923760309EA764420987

O'Flaherty, J., & Phillips, C. (2015). The use of flipped classrooms in higher education: A scoping review. *The Internet and Higher Education, 25*, 85–95. http://dx.doi.org/10.1016/j.iheduc.2015.02.002

O'Keeffe, M., & Donnelly, R. (2013). Exploration of ePortfolios for adding value and deepening student learning in contemporary higher education. *International Journal of ePortfolio, 3*(1), 1–11. Retrieved from http://www.theijep.com/pdf/IJEP92.pdf

Oliver, R. (2000, December). When teaching meets learning: Design principles and strategies for web-based learning environments that support knowledge construction. *ASCILITE 2000 Online Papers*. Retrieved from http://www.ascilite.org/conferences/coffs00/papers/ron_oliver_keynote.pdf

Omnicore. (2018, September 5). YouTube by the numbers: Stats, demographics & fun facts. Retrieved from https://www.omnicoreagency.com/youtube-statistics/

OpenStax. (2019). Improving access, learning, and our world [Website content]. Houston, Tex.: Rice University. Retrieved from https://openstax.org/impact

O'Reilly, T. (2005, September 30). What is Web 2.0? [Blog post]. Retrieved from https://www.oreilly.com/pub/a/web2/archive/what-is-web-20.html

Orlowski, A. (2018, November 30). Blockchain study finds 0.00% success rate and vendors don't call back when asked for evidence. *The Register*. Retrieved from https://www.theregister.co.uk/2018/11/30/blockchain_study_finds_0_per_cent_success_rate/

Orr, D, Weller, M., & Farrow, R. (2018). *Models for online, open, flexible and technology enhanced higher education across the globe — a comparative analysis*. Oslo, Norway: International Council for Distance Education. Retrieved from http://oro.open.ac.uk/55299/1/Models-report-April-2018.pdf

Pane, J., Steiner, E., Baird, M., Hamilton, L., & Pane, J. (2017). *Informing progress: Insights on personalized learning implementation and effects*. Santa Monica, CA: RAND Corporation. Retrieved from https://www.rand.org/pubs/research_reports/RR2042.html.

Pappano, L. (2012, November 14). The year of the MOOC. *New York Times*. Retrieved from https://www.nytimes.com/2012/11/04/education/edlife/massive-open-online-courses-are-multiplying-at-a-rapid-pace.html?mtrref=undefined&gwh=FC7A15458E07C02EB2F19B97005DAA0E&gwt=pay&assetType=REGIWALL

Parr, S. (2012, March 30). We know our education system is broken, so why can't we fix it? *Fast Company*. Retrieved from https://www.fastcompany.com/1826287/we-know-our-education-system-broken-so-why-cant-we-fix-it

Perryman, L-A., Law, P., & Law, A. (2013). Developing sustainable business models for institutions' provision of open educational resources: Learning from OpenLearn users' motivations and experiences. In *Open and Flexible Higher Education Conference 2013* (pp. 270–286). Paris, France: European Association of Distance Teaching Universities. Retrieved from http://oro.open.ac.uk/39101/1/eadtu%20annual%20conference%202013%20-%20proceedings.pdf

Phipps, L. (2018, December 19). Mind the gap! [Blog post]. Retrieved from http://lawriephipps.co.uk/?p=8940

Piaget, J. (1964). Part I: Cognitive development in children: Piaget development and learning. *Journal of Research in Science Teaching*, 2(3), 176–186. https://doi.org/10.1002/tea.3660020306

Pickard, L. (2018, February 6). TU Delft students can earn credit for M O O C s from other universities [Blog post]. *Class Central*. Retrieved from https://www. class-central.com/report/delft-virtual-exchange-program/

Pollock, G. (1988). *Vision and difference: Femininity, feminism, and histories of art.* London, U K: Routledge.

Publishers Association. (2016). *PA publishing yearbook 2016.* London, U K: Publishers Association.

Raish, V., & Rimland, E. (2016). Employer perceptions of critical information literacy skills and digital badges. *College & Research Libraries, 77*(1), 87–113. https:// doi.org/10.5860/crl.77.1.87

Raith, A. (2011, August 23). Stanford for everyone: More than 120,000 enroll in free classes. *KQED News*. Retrieved from https://www.kqed.org/mindshift/14740/ stanford-for-everyone-more-than-120000-enroll-in-free-classes

Rakes, G.C. (1996). Using the Internet as a tool in a resource-based learning environment. *Educational Technology, 36*(5), 52–56.

Reed, A. (2017, December 22). The environmental impacts of bitcoin. *Wolverine Blockchain*. Retrieved from https://medium.com/wolverineblockchain/the-environmental-impacts-of-bitcoin-b01592b8c848

Rees, J. (2014). The flipped classroom is decadent and depraved [Blog post]. *More or Less Bunk*. Retrieved from https://moreorlessbunk.wordpress.com/2014/05/05/ the-flipped-classroom-is-decadent-and-depraved/?

Rienties, B. (2018, October). L T I series—Learning analytics with Bart Rienties. *IN SlideShare*. Retrieved from https://www.slideshare.net/BartRienties/ lti-series-learning-analytics-with-bart-rienties

Rigg, P. (2014, October 31). Can universities survive the digital age? *University World News*. Retrieved from https://www.universityworldnews.com/post. php?story=20141030125107100

Roll, I., & Wylie, R. (2016). Evolution and revolution in artificial intelligence in education. *International Journal of Artificial Intelligence in Education, 26* (2), 582–599. https://doi.org/10.1007/s40593-016-0110-3

Russell, T.L. (1999). *The no significant difference phenomenon: As reported in 355 research reports, summaries and papers.* Raleigh, NC: North Carolina State University.

Salmon, G. (2004). *E-moderating: The key to online teaching and learning.* New York, N Y: Routledge.

Sanford, K., Merkel, L., & Madill, L. (2011). There's no fixed course: Rhizomatic learning communities in adolescent videogaming. *Loading...The Journal of the Canadian Game Studies Association, 5*(8), 50–70.

Schlusmans, K., van den Munckhof, R., & Nielissen, G. (2017). Active online education: A new educational approach at the Open Universiteit of the Netherlands. In G. Ubachs & L. Konings (Eds.), *Conference proceedings: The online, open, and higher education conference* (pp. 54–70). Maastricht, The Netherlands: E A D T U. Retrieved from https://conference.eadtu.eu/download2399

Sclater, N. (2014). Learning analytics: The current state of play in UK higher and further education. *Jisc*. Retrieved from http://repository.jisc.ac.uk/5657/1/Learning_analytics_report.pdf

Sclater, N., & Mullan, J. (2017). Learning analytics and student success–Assessing the evidence. *Jisc briefing*. Retrieved from https://repository.jisc.ac.uk/6560/1/learning-analytics_and_student_success.pdf

Sclater, N., Peasgood, A., & Mullan, J. (2016). Learning analytics in higher education: A review of UK and international practice. *Jisc report*. Retrieved from https://www.jisc.ac.uk/reports/learning-analytics-in-higher-education

Seaman, J., & Seaman, J. (2017). *Opening the textbook: Educational resources in U.S. higher education, 2017*. Babson Park, MA: Babson Survey Research Group.

Seaman, J., & Seaman, J. (2018) *Freeing the textbook: Educational resources in U.S. higher education, 2018*. Babson Park, MA: Babson Survey Research Group.

Selwyn, N. (2014). Data entry: Towards the critical study of digital data and education. *Learning, Media and Technology*, 40(1), 64–82. https://dx.doi.org/10.1080/17439884.2014.921628

Selwyn, N. (2018, June 12). Six reasons artificial intelligence technology will never take over from human teachers [Blog post]. *EduResearch Matters*. Retrieved from https://www.aare.edu.au/blog/?p=2948

Sharma, M. (2008). *Elgg social networking*. Birmingham, UK: Packt Publishing.

Shirky, C. (2008). *Here comes everybody: The power of organizing without organizations*. New York, NY: Penguin.

Shirky, C. (2012, December 17). Higher education: Our MP3 is the mooc. *The Guardian*. Retrieved from https://www.theguardian.com/education/2012/dec/17/moocs-higher-education-transformation

Siemens, G. (2005). Connectivism: A learning theory for the digital age. Retrieved from http://er.dut.ac.za/bitstream/handle/123456789/69/Siemens_2005_Connectivism_A_learning_theory_for_the_digital_age.pdf

Siemens, G., & Long, P. (2011). Penetrating the fog: Analytics in learning and education. *EDUCAUSE Review*, 46(5). Retrieved from https://er.educause.edu/articles/2011/9/penetrating-the-fog-analytics-in-learning-and-education

Silverman, R. (2016, February 17). Bosses tap outside firms to predict which workers might get sick. *Wall Street Journal*. Retrieved from https://www.wsj.com/articles/bosses-harness-big-data-to-predict-which-workers-might-get-sick-1455664940

Simpson, O. (2004). Access, retention and course choice in online, open and distance learning. *European Journal of Open, Distance and E-learning*, 7(1). Retrieved from http://www.eurodl.org/materials/contrib/2004/Ormond_Simpson.pdf

Singh, O., & Ritzhaupt, A. (2006). Student perspective of organizational uses of ePortfolios in higher education. In E. Pearson & P. Bohman (Eds.), *EdMedia: World conference on educational media and technology* (pp. 1717–1722). Waynesville, NC: Association for the Advancement of Computing in Education (AACE). Retrieved from http://www.aritzhaupt.com/eprofessional/papers/2006/SinghRitzhaupt.pdf

Skinner, B.F. (1963). Operant behavior. *American Psychologist, 18*(8), 503. http://dx.doi.org/10.1037/h0045185

Slade, S., & Prinsloo, P. (2013). Learning analytics: Ethical issues and dilemmas. *American Behavioral Scientist, 57*(10), 1510–1529. https://doi.org/10.1177/0002764213479366

Smits, P., Verbeek, J., & de Buisonjé, C. (2002). Problem-based learning in continuing medical education: A review of controlled evaluation studies. *British Medical Journal, 324*(7330), 153–156. https://doi.org/10.1136/bmj.324.7330.153

Spiro, R.J., Feltovich, P.J., Feltovich, P.L., Jacobson, M.J., & Coulson, R.L. (1991). Cognitive flexibility, constructivism, and hypertext: Random access instruction for advanced knowledge acquisition in ill-structured domains. *Educational Technology, 31*(5), 24–33.

Staton, M. (2012). Disaggregating the components of a college degree. American Enterprise Institute, Washington, D C. Retrieved from http://www.aei.org/wp-content/uploads/2012/08/-disaggregating-the-components-of-a-college-degree_184521175818.pdf

Stewart, B. (2015). Open to influence: What counts as academic influence in scholarly networked Twitter participation. *Learning, Media and Technology, 40*(3), 287–309. https://doi.org/10.1080/17439884.2015.1015547

Stewart, B. (2016). Collapsed publics: Orality, literacy, and vulnerability in academic Twitter. *Journal of Applied Social Theory, 1*(1). Retrieved from https://social-theoryapplied.com/journal/jast/article/view/33/9

Straumsheim, C. (2013, December 18). Scaling back in San Jose. *Inside Higher Ed*. Retrieved from https://www.insidehighered.com/news/2013/12/18/san-jose-state-u-resurrects-scaled-back-online-course-experiment-mooc-provider

Tapscott, D., & Tapscott, A. (2016). *Blockchain revolution: How the technology behind bitcoin is changing money, business, and the world*. New York, N Y: Penguin.

Techcrunch. (2009, February 14). Web 2.0 is dead. Retrieved from https://techcrunch.com/2009/02/14/the-death-of-web-20/

Thomas, A. (2018). Twenty years on the edge: Keynote at A L T - C 2018. Retrieved from https://fragmentsofamber.wordpress.com/2018/09/12/altc2018/

Thomas, A., Campbell, L., Barker P., & Hawksey, M. (2012). *Into the wild – Technology for open educational resources*. Bolton, U K: University of Bolton. Retrieved from http://publications.cetis.org.uk/wp-content/uploads/2012/12/into_the_wild_screen.pdf

Tufecki, Z. (2018, March 10). YouTube, the great radicalizer. *The New York Times*. Retrieved from https://www.nytimes.com/2018/03/10/opinion/sunday/youtube-politics-radical.html

U K L O M Core. (2003). United Kingdom Learning Object Metadata Core [Report]. Retrieved from http://zope.cetis.ac.uk/profiles/uklomcore/

U N E S C O. (2012a). 2012 Paris O E R declaration. Retrieved from https://unesdoc.unesco.org/ark:/48223/pf0000246687

U N E S C O. (2012b). Open Educational Resources (O E R). Retrieved from https://en.unesco.org/themes/building-knowledge-societies/oer

UNESCO. (2018). DRAFT text 18 April 2018 — Recommendation on Open Educational Resources (OER). Retrieved from https://www.oercongress.org/wp-content/uploads/2018/04/Draft-OER-Recommendation-Version-Draft-18-April-2018-text-for-online-consultation-ENG.pdf

Van Harmelen, M. (2006). Personal learning environments. In *Proceedings of the Sixth International Conference on Advanced Learning Technologies (ICALT'06)* (pp. 815–816). IEEE. Retrieved from http://citeseerx.ist.psu.edu/viewdoc/download?doi=10.1.1.97.2772&rep=rep1&type=pdf

Veletsianos, G., & Kimmons, R. (2012). Networked participatory scholarship: Emergent techno-cultural pressures toward open and digital scholarship in online networks. *Computers & Education, 58*(2), 766–774. Retrieved from https://www.veletsianos.com/wp-content/uploads/2011/11/NPS_final_published.pdf

Vernon, D., & Blake R.L. (1993). Does problem based learning work? A meta analysis of evaluation research. *Academic Medicine, 68*(7), 550–563. http://dx.doi.org/10.1097/00001888-199307000-00015

Vincent, J. (2018, October 10). Amazon reportedly scraps internal AI recruiting tool that was biased against women. *The Verge.* Retrieved from https://www.theverge.com/2018/10/10/17958784/ai-recruiting-tool-bias-amazon-report

Virgin.com. (2015). Disruptors 2015–The future of education: Does the current model make the grade? [Website content]. Retrieved from https://www.virgin.com/disruptors/disruptors-2015-future-education-does-current-model-make-grade

Vygotsky, L.S. (1978). *Mind in society: The development of higher psychological processes.* Cambridge, MA: Harvard University Press.

Wagner, C. (2006). Breaking the knowledge acquisition bottleneck through conversational knowledge management. *Information Resources Management Journal, 19*(1), 70–83. Retrieved from https://www.igi-global.com/gateway/article/full-text-pdf/1286

Watters, A. (2013a, May 24). The myth and the millennialism of disruptive innovation. Retrieved from http://hackeducation.com/2013/05/24/disruptive-innovation

Watters, A. (2013b). Zombie ideas (Ed-tech ideas that refuse to die even though we know they're monstrous). Retrieved from http://2013trends.hackeducation.com/zombies.html

Watters, A. (2016, August 23). A domain of one's own in a post-ownership society. Retrieved from http://hackeducation.com/2016/08/23/domains

Watters, A. (2017, November 1). AI is ideological. *New Internationalist.* Retrieved from https://newint.org/features/2017/11/01/audrey-watters-ai

Watters, A. (2018a, April 5). What are the best books about the history of education technology? Retrieved from http://hackeducation.com/2018/04/05/history-of-education-technology

Watters, A. (2018b, December 18). The stories we were told about education technology. Retrieved from http://hackeducation.com/2018/12/18/top-ed-tech-trends-stories

Weber, J. S. (1995). Defining cyberlibel: A first amendment limit for libel suits against individuals arising from computer bulletin board speech. *Case Western Reserve Law Review, 46*(1), 235–278. Retrieved from https://scholarlycommons.law.case.edu/caselrev/vol46/iss1/7/

Webster, C. A. G., Weller, M., Sfantsikopoulos, M. M., & Tsoukalas, V. D. (1993). ALEXSYS —A prototype knowledge based expert system for the quality assurance of high pressure die castings. In *International Conference on Database and Expert Systems Applications* (pp. 396–400). Berlin, Germany: Springer.

Weinberger, D. (2007). *Everything is miscellaneous: The power of the new digital disorder.* New York, NY: Times Books.

Weller, M. (2000). Creating a large-scale, third generation, distance education course. *Open Learning: The Journal of Open, Distance and e-Learning, 15*(3), 243–252. http://dx.doi.org/10.1080/713688403

Weller, M. (2004). Models of large scale e-learning. *Journal of Asynchronous Learning Networks, 8*(4), 83–92.

Weller, M. (2007a, November 14). Blogs easier to read than formal publications [Blog post]. *The Ed Techie.* Retrieved from http://blog.edtechie.net/weblogs/blogs-easier-to/

Weller, M. (2007b). Learning objects, learning design, and adoption through succession. *Journal of Computing in Higher Education, 19*(1), 26–47.

Weller, M. (2007c). *Virtual learning environments: Using, choosing and developing your VLE.* Oxford, UK: Routledge.

Weller, M. (2007d, November 8). The VLE is dead [Blog post]. *The Ed Techie.* Retrieved from http://blog.edtechie.net/web-2-0/the-vlelms-is-d/

Weller, M. (2011). A pedagogy of abundance. *Spanish Journal of Pedagogy, 249,* 223–236.

Weller, M. (2012, April 29). The virtues of blogging as scholarly activity. *The Chronicle of Higher Education.* Retrieved from https://www.chronicle.com/article/The-Virtues-of-Blogging-as/131666

Weller, M. (2014). *The battle for Open: How openness won and why it doesn't feel like victory.* London, UK: Ubiquity Press.

Weller, M. (2016a). Different aspects of the emerging OER discipline. *Revista Educacao e Cultura Contemporanea, 13*(31), 404–418. Retrieved from http://periodicos.estacio.br/index.php/reeduc/article/view/2321/1171

Weller, M. (2016b). The Open flip–a digital economic model for education. *Journal of Learning for Development, 3*(2), 26–34.

Weller, M., de los Arcos, B., Farrow, R., Pitt, B, & McAndrew, P. (2015). The impact of OER on teaching and learning practice. *Open Praxis, 7*(4), 351–361.

Weller, M., Jordan, K., DeVries, I., & Rolfe, V. (2018). Mapping the open education landscape: Citation network analysis of historical open and distance education research. *Open Praxis, 10*(2), 109–126.

Wenger, E. (1998). *Communities of practice: Learning, meaning, and identity.* Cambridge, UK: Cambridge University Press.

Wesch, M. (2008, July 10). *A portal on media literacy* [Video file]. Retrieved from http://www.youtube.com/watch?v=J4yApagnros

Wikipedia. (2017). Writing Wikipedia articles course [Website content]. Retrieved from https://en.wikipedia.org/wiki/Wikipedia:Writing_Wikipedia_Articles_course

Wild, J. (2012). OER engagement study: Promoting OER reuse among academics. Research report from the SCORE funded project. Retrieved from https://ora.ox.ac.uk/objects/uuid:eca4f8cd-edf5-4b38-a9b0-4dd2d4e59750/

Wiley, D. (2002). The reusability paradox. http://opencontent.org/docs/paradox.html

Wiley, D. (2008, January 20). Social objects and campfires [Blog post]. Retrieved from https://opencontent.org/blog/archives/437

Wiley, D. (2009, June 10). Dark matter, dark reuse, and the irrational zeal of a believer [Blog post]. Retrieved from https://opencontent.org/blog/archives/905

Wiley, D. (2013, October 21). What is open pedagogy? [Blog post]. Retrieved from https://opencontent.org/blog/archives/2975

Wiley, D., & Hilton III, J. (2018). Defining OER-enabled pedagogy. *The International Review of Research in Open and Distributed Learning, 19*(4). http://dx.doi.org/10.19173/irrodl.v19i4.3601

Wilson, S., Liber, O., Johnson, M., Beauvoir, P., Sharples, P., & Milligan, C. (2007). Personal learning environments: Challenging the dominant design of educational systems. *Journal of E-learning and Knowledge Society, 3*(2), 27–38.

Wood, D.J., Bruner, J.S., & Ross, G. (1976). The role of tutoring in problem solving. *Journal of Child Psychiatry and Psychology, 17*(2), 89–100.

Worth, J. (2015). *Innovative pedagogies series: Synthesising approaches to openness.* York, UK: Higher Education Academy. https://www.heacademy.ac.uk/system/files/jonathan_worth_final.pdf

Zittrain, J.L. (2006). The generative internet. *Harvard Law Review, 119*, 1974–2040. Retrieved from https://dash.harvard.edu/bitstream/handle/1/9385626/zittrain_generativeinternet.pdf?sequence=1

Zuckerberg, M. (2017, December 13). Lessons in philanthropy 2017 [Facebook post]. Retrieved from https://www.facebook.com/notes/mark-zuckerberg/lessons-in-philanthropy-2017/10155543109576634/

ABOUT THE AUTHOR

MARTIN WELLER is the director of The Open Education Research Hub and the director of the GO-GN network. Weller chaired the Open University's first major online e-learning course in 1999, which attracted 15,000 students, and was the OU's first LMS Director. His popular blog, edtechie.net features his writings on aspects of educational technology. He is the author of *The Battle for Open* (2014) and *The Digital Scholar* (2011).